Language, Ideology, and Totalitarianism

Rereading Orwell's 1984 in the Context of Trump's Presidency

SHAFQAT MUSHTAQ

Kashmir Stag Imprints

ISBN: 9798224608386

CONTENTS

ACKNOWLEDGMENTS

It would immensely be unjust not to thank friends and family for their unwavering support: thank you for being with me through the thick and thin of writing this book!

PREFACE

This book, "Language, Ideology, and Totalitarianism," delves deeply into the mechanisms of totalitarianism. It examines how totalitarian regimes operate, how they disseminate their divisive ideologies, and how language serves as a tool to undermine critical thinking and foster blind conformity. To illustrate these points, the discussion draws on the Trump presidency and George Orwell's '1984,' showing how the policies pursued and linguistic manipulations in '1984's' Oceania and Trump's America share striking similarities.

George Orwell's 1984 continues to be a must-read, as it addresses humanity's current social, political, and cultural challenges. This dynamic analysis examines the relevance of Orwell's dystopian and prescient novel in current political circumstances, presenting a horrific picture of a totalitarian society plagued by manipulation of language, blatant governmental control, constant and severe state surveillance, distortion of history for political ends, and the rise of fascism.

While the title 'post-Trump context' implies that Trump is a lone 'autocratic leader' and solely responsible for the brazen distortion of reality, it is important to note that this is not the case. Instead, this book aims to demonstrate how totalitarianism pursues certain policies and how Trump's election has contributed to an unprecedented rise in the pursuit of those disruptive and divisive policies.

The fear of public retribution and outcry has become irrelevant, and divisive policies are being pursued with immense state force. Propaganda and news have become one, and politics now rules over the minds of people. Voices of intellect and sanity are being apprehended in the same manner as criminals and fugitives.

I firmly believe that compared to poor and weak democratic countries, America is still in a better position. However, this does not excuse Trump's Orwellian tendencies. If he was restrained, it is not necessarily an indication of his good intentions, but rather a testament to the strength of institutional integrity, active civil society, and free press, which have managed to withstand the assault on democracy and freedom.

However, the situation in weak democracies is quite the opposite, where institutional degradation is rampant. There is a worrying erosion of democracy and press freedom, with only the state narrative being telecasted across hundreds of news channels. Social media platforms like WhatsApp are being used to spread fake news and propaganda, while alternative voices are being suppressed.

Autocrats tend to create their own version of reality, which they then force upon others. Similarly, Trump is so deeply immersed in his own constructed reality that the concept of *"objective reality"* holds no significance for him as long as he can convince enough people to believe in his falsehoods.[1] Such leaders believe in the ultimate authority of their own words, which cannot be disputed or overridden, similar to fascists. This mindset can have perilous consequences, especially when leaders enjoy popular support and a parliamentary majority, leading to personal aspirations taking precedence over people's aspirations.

The brazen attempt to spread deception by manipulating language has far-reaching consequences, as it creates an information vacuum and opens the door for falsehoods and rumors to flourish.

Adam Gopnik in his New Yorker article titled Orwell's "1984" and Trump's America puts it eloquently:

"There is nothing subtle about Trump's behavior. He lies, he repeats the lie, and his listeners either cower in fear, stammer in disbelief, or try to see how they can turn the lie to their own benefit."[2]

The purpose of fabricating lies is to sustain the conversation until they are perceived as legitimate options worthy of inclusion in public discourse. Instances of such behavior can be observed

---

[1] Jack Holmes, Trump's War on the Truth Has Officially Gone Full Orwell - Esquire (https://www.esquire.com/news-politics/a22547037/donald-trump-orwellian-truth-reality-eyes-ears/)

[2] Adam Gopnik, Orwell's "1984" and Trump's America - The New Yorker (https://www.newyorker.com/news/daily-comment/orwells-1984-and-trumps-america)

worldwide, be it in India, America, the Middle East, Africa, Europe or any other place. In India, for example, we witness the rewriting of history to serve certain agendas, portraying one community in a favorable light while falsely vilifying others.

In both Trump's America and India today, politics thrives on the rejection of truth and the mockery of logic. With the support of compliant media and social media cells, people are all too willing to accept these lies. Shivam Vij writes in The Print:

"The Modi government has made lying an art form. This non-stop obvious lying was described by George Orwell as doublethink. People are thus expected to believe as true what is clearly false, and also take at face value mutually contradictory statements. The Modi government talked about NRC, but it also did not talk about it."[3]

Despite factual evidence presented, people who are continuously exposed to lies become convinced to believe nothing at all. Trump refused to accept Biden's win in Arizona, even after a "full forensic audit" showed that not only did Biden win, but his vote share was more than earlier recorded. Trump dismissed the audit as "fake news." Trump's followers are conditioned to only believe what their leader tells them, causing them to be distrustful of any information that conflicts with what Trump

---

[3] Why The Modi Government Gets Away With Lies, And How The Opposition Could Change That - The Print (https://theprint.in/opinion/why-modi-government-gets-away-with-lies/422211/)

says.[4]

As we witness the catastrophe that George Orwell prophesied in 1984, his book has become a must-read for the 21st century readers. Orwell's work offers a prescient warning about the dangers of totalitarianism, government control, and the suppression of freedom. His novel's relevance in the post-Trump context is undeniable, as we witness the rise of authoritarian regimes and the erosion of democratic values. It is up to us to heed Orwell's warning and fight for a future that is free from the dystopian reality that he so aptly described.

***

Decades after its publication, Orwell's 1984 remains a cautionary tale to criticize leaders for their fascist actions. In the aftermath of 9/11, George W. Bush's administration engaged in state-sponsored oppression that bore a striking resemblance to the dystopian world of 1984. Similarly, Barack Obama's secret surveillance project conducted by the NSA drew comparisons to the novel's themes of government overreach and

---

[4] Neil Steinberg, 'The news is all lies anyway' - Chicago Sun Times (https://chicago.suntimes.com/columnists/2021/9/28/22698177/orwell-1984-trump-fake-news-arizona-audit-elections-georgia-steinberg)

the erosion of individual privacy.

Former Vice President Al Gore's criticism of President Bush's "war on terror" is prophetic and remains relevant today. Gore saw the "war on terror" as a ploy to "rule by secrecy and unquestioned authority," warning that it could "take [America] farther down the road toward an intrusive, Big Brother-style government."[5] By wielding unchecked power in the name of national security, civil liberties are suspended and restricted access to information creates a culture of fear and suspicion. Gore's criticism is a vital reminder of the need for checks and balances to prevent abuses of power.

The rise of illiberal democracies and military dictatorships worldwide is a worrying trend that threatens to undermine democracy. Unfortunately, India, which has been grappling with its own brand of "autocratic rule," is not immune to this trend. This is particularly concerning for a country with a population of over 1.3 billion and an economy that is currently spiraling downward. Instead of focusing on economic issues, impoverished voters are increasingly swayed by the rhetoric of nationalism. This can have serious repercussions, especially when *over 12 million people enter the workforce every year.*[6]

---

[5] Hunter Schwarz, CNN, Sales are Spiking for '1984,' But it has a Long History in Politics
(https://edition.cnn.com/2017/01/26/politics/politics-of-1984-through-the-years/index.html)
[6] Narendra Modi is India's Trump - The Washington Post
(https://www.washingtonpost.com/opinions/2019/11/13/naren

The government's inability to tackle economic challenges has been overshadowed by the constant propaganda from allied newsrooms, resulting in the redirection of public frustration towards elites and minorities.

Totalitarian regimes operate by suppressing access to factual information, fearing that such information may expose their true motives and lead people to question their authority. They do not support the idea of unbiased information without filters, as this would increase people's tolerance levels, which is not in line with their agenda. Instead, intolerance and fear are more suitable for their purposes. Therefore, citizens must take responsibility for gathering as much information as possible and making informed decisions about their political choices. It is also crucial that people understand the workings of totalitarianism, and reading books about it can be helpful in this regard.

Orwell's warning against "blissful ignorance" reminds us of the importance of staying aware and well-informed. Totalitarian regimes rely on keeping their populations deluded and distracted to the extent that they reject the truth outright.

In "1984," Big Brother achieved this control by "spreading false rumors and eliminating dissenting individuals." By stoking patriotism, Big Brother made "longer working hours or scarce rations"[7]

---

dra-modi-is-indias-trump/)
[7] NATELEGÉ WHALEY, '1984' Book: Here are 4 Eerie Similarities

appear justifiable to the masses. It is our responsibility to recognize these tactics and resist the manipulation of truth and reality.

The events such as the Women's March on Washington, Black Lives Matter protests, millions of farmers protesting in India against farm laws, and anti-CAA protests across India show that many people are aware and not easily distracted, and they oppose what they deem as anti-democratic and anti-secular moves by the government.

As I conclude, I want to leave you with this impactful quote from George Orwell:

"The totalitarian state creates an ideology for you, it tries to govern your emotional life as well as setting up a code of conduct. And as far as possible it isolates you from the outside world, it shuts you up in an artificial universe in which you have no standards of comparison."[8]

to Trump's America - MIC (https://www.mic.com/articles/166589/1984-book-here-are-4-e erie-similarities-to-trump-s-america)

[8] John Avlon, Tiananmen, Orwell and Trump - CNN (https://edition.cnn.com/2019/06/04/opinions/tiananmen-orw ell-trump-avlon/index.html)

Introduction

If you haven't read George Orwell's 1984 yet, this brief overview of the novel can offer valuable context and help deepen your understanding of the themes explored in this book. Additionally, for a more detailed summary, you can refer to Chapter 13, titled "A Brief Chapter Wise Summary of 1984". This chapter will provide a comprehensive summary of the novel, helping you better understand the storyline and its underlying themes.

George Orwell's "1984" is a dystopian novel that takes place in a totalitarian society where the government, known as "the Party," has complete control over every aspect of people's lives. The story follows the life of Winston Smith, a low-ranking member of the Party who works as a government clerk in the Ministry of Truth, where his job is to rewrite history to fit the Party's propaganda.

Winston is disillusioned with the Party and secretly rebels against it by keeping a diary, which is a *thoughtcrime* punishable by death. Winston's growing discontent with the Party is heightened when he meets a woman named Julia, with whom he begins a secret love affair.

Throughout the novel, Orwell explores themes of totalitarianism, oppression, manipulation, and the power of language. One of the most striking aspects of the novel is the way in which the Party manipulates language to control people's thoughts and behaviors. The Party has created a new language called *Newspeak*, which is designed to limit people's ability to express themselves and eliminate dissenting voices.

Orwell also explores the role of technology in the Party's control over society. The Party uses *telescreens* to monitor people's every move and to disseminate its propaganda. The telescreens are also used to enforce the Party's strict regulations, such as the prohibition on private thought.

Winston's rebellion against the Party ultimately leads to his capture and torture by the Party's agents. In the novel's climax, Winston is brainwashed into loving Big Brother, the Party's leader, and he accepts the Party's view of reality without question.

"1984" is a powerful critique of totalitarianism and a warning about the dangers of government control. The novel presents a chilling vision of a world in which people's thoughts and emotions are completely subordinated to the will of the government. Orwell's portrayal of a society in which language is manipulated and dissent is punished reflects his own experiences as a writer and political commentator during a time of great upheaval and political instability.

The novel has had a profound influence on popular culture and political discourse, and many of its concepts and phrases, such as "Big Brother," "thoughtcrime" and "doublethink," have become part of the lexicon of political discourse. The novel's message remains as relevant today as it was when it was first published in 1949, and it continues to be studied and discussed by scholars and readers around the world.

"1984" is a thought-provoking and deeply disturbing novel that presents a vision of a totalitarian society in which individual freedom and autonomy have been completely eliminated. The novel's exploration of themes such as government control, manipulation of language, and the dangers of technology continues to resonate with readers today, and it remains a powerful critique of the potential dangers of unchecked state power. Orwell's vision of a society in which people are completely subordinated to the will of the government serves as a warning about the dangers of totalitarianism and a call to vigilance against any attempts to erode individual freedom and autonomy.

To readers who rely on books to make sense of the world around them ...

Language, Ideology, and Totalitarianism

1
1984: Dystopian Classic to Amazon Bestseller

Never before in the history of literature have dystopian novels been read with such widespread interest as they are now. Following the election of Donald Trump as the President of the United States, readers have renewed their fascination with dystopian literature. However, there is a stark difference in how dystopia is perceived now compared to in the past.

In the past, dystopian literature was seen as a product of wild imagination that was far removed from real-life scenarios. It was akin to finding a new abode on another planet and observing, from a position of comfortable detachment, as the earth was destroyed due to an imbalance in its delicate environmental balance caused by anthropogenic activities and totalitarian regimes wreaking havoc on its political fabric.

The ability of readers to suspend reality while

being immersed in the imaginary has been a characteristic of dystopian literature. However, this luxury is no longer available to modern readers.

There is no sense of detachment when reading George Orwell's dystopian novel, 1984. Instead, readers are left feeling as if they are living through the catastrophe unfolding in the book, with a keen sense of the imminence and urgency of the doom. Consequently, at the end of the book, they are left with a terrible feeling of anxiety and disheartening bitterness, as they realize that yesterday's dystopia is today's reality. There is no comfort or consolation for the modern reader as their world is turned upside down. They come to realize that what they are reading is not the same as what they have been coerced into believing is the real world. This chasm between the real and the imagined, the actual and the simulated, creates an uncanny tension that is distressing, as readers come to realize they are being robbed of the truth.

This marks a despairing shift in the history of literature. Consider Don Quixote, which is based on sheer fancy and chivalric romance far removed from external reality as experienced in everyday life. In sharp contrast, today's fiction is the ultimate fact as it rips apart the veiled web of deceptions to present reality in its stark nakedness.

The constant stream of propaganda peddled through mass media with malicious intent to keep the masses deluded has constricted the space for truth. The only safe outlet for truth is the medium of fiction. In an era where it is humanly impossible to separate propaganda and fake news from the truth because they have been so intertwined, just the sheer volume of it is so overwhelming that it is hard to care anymore about reading between the lines.

It is in this context that George Orwell's 1984 has remained relevant and continued to top bestseller lists, even decades after its publication. One of the reasons that 1984 is considered one of the greatest works in the history of literature is its prophetic depiction of the cultural, political, and economic future of humankind in the coming decades.

George Orwell's dystopian novel, 1984, presents a prescient warning of impending doom resulting from totalitarian government control, pervasive state surveillance, manipulation of language and history for political gains, and the unchecked growth of fascism.

Regardless of the political system in power, the pursuit of disruptive policies has become a common feature worldwide. The fear of public retribution and outcry no longer deters the political class from executing their divisive agendas.

If anything, such policies are being pursued with immense state power, even if that means suppressing voices of reason and treating dissenters as criminals and fugitives. This is reminiscent of the world that George Orwell prophesied in 1984, making it a must-read for those who want to better understand the times we live in the 21st century.

***

Contrary to some beliefs that books have lost their allure and readers' interest, the trend is quite the opposite. Today, there are more avid readers than were ever in the history of literature. Readers are willing to go to great lengths to find that one book that will leave them with timeless wisdom and insights, while also adding to their bookshelves with profound philosophies.

It's not just modern publications that are gaining popularity, but classical books as well. And for good reason - there's a certain profundity to these works that resonate with readers. While modern publications can often be filled with triviality and sporadic philosophical outbursts, it's the classics that continue to rule the roost. This is exemplified by the enduring popularity of George Orwell's dystopian novel, 1984, which has not only made it to the Amazon bestseller list but also topped many must-read lists in recent years.

What propelled readers to read and reread 1984, and what makes it feel like it was published just yesterday? Perhaps it's the fact that modern readers can relate to the prevalence of totalitarian regimes, which has become the political reality of our times. 1984 isn't just a bundle of ink-smeared pages bound together; it's an alarm bell warning of an impending human tragedy. Orwell's all-hearing and all-seeing

Big Brother has been replaced by today's technological deities, such as surveillance states and apparatuses, who have absolute knowledge of their subjects and have reduced them to mere objects. In the novel, 1984, homes are bugged with listening devices, not as instruments of convenience, but as eavesdroppers listening in on people's conversations and reporting back to Big Brother. George Orwell's predicted world is devoid of human compassion, instead overflowing with hatred and hysteria.

He presents a horrifying picture of a world where crime and propaganda are the only reality of government and state with utmost vividness. Propaganda is fabricated daily to keep the masses deluded and subjected, and to influence public opinion. The media is hand in glove with state machinery to ignite sentiments of hyper-nationalism, far-right ideology, and military jingoism, and spews venom to disturb social harmony, eschewing inclusiveness for divisiveness. In this world, loss is omnipresent and George Orwell paints this picture with stark clarity.

The rise of 1984 to the No. 1 spot on Amazon was attributed to Kellyanne Conway's assertion in an NBC interview that the Trump administration was providing *"alternative facts"* about the size of the crowd at Trump's inauguration. This claim drew comparisons to the concept of "doublespeak" in George Orwell's dystopian classic. In response, people took to Twitter, and Penguin, the publisher of 1984, seized the opportunity by announcing a reprint of 75,000 copies. With the election of Trump, volunteers, philanthropists, and businessmen purchased more copies of the novel to distribute among the public, highlighting the dangers of totalitarianism's manipulation of language and truth.

The regime's inclination to "control the narrative" is a troubling sign as it substitutes truth with lies, facts with fantasy, and comprehension with bewilderment. Such a trend ultimately leads to a world where, as Winston Smith, the protagonist of Nineteen Eighty-Four, puts it, they *"would announce that two and two made five, and you would have to believe it."*

If it means censoring critical thinking and objective truth, the regime would go to any length to nip them in the bud. It would deploy *"thought police"* to *track and eliminate* any revolutionary impulse and *"unperson"* citizens until all rational thought is not just purged, but fully replaced with party propaganda. Orwell identified *emotional nationalism* and the denial of *objective truth* as means of political subjugation and exploitation. Trump's rhetoric about immigrants snatching American jobs and calling "climate change a Chinese hoax" is alarming, as it is an outrageous denial of facts.

'1984' isn't emblematic of Trump's way of politics alone. Obama's surveillance project, which he kept secret from the public, is also Orwellian. What he did was similar to what Big Brother would do in the '1984' novel, which is listening in secretly to people's communications via telescreens.

In other words, the dystopia portrayed in Orwell's works is not limited to a specific individual, political party, or country. (Although Trump's presidency in the United States was so deeply reminiscent of the Orwellian dystopia that it's difficult to imagine a better example.) It's a universal desire for control and authority that transcends party lines, whether it be Democrats or Republicans, Left or Right, Socialists or Communists, and it can only be achieved through the use of technology and language to manipulate the thoughts and behaviors of the masses.

'1984' depicts a terrifying world that is difficult to comprehend. It is a world where access to genuine history is forbidden, where political language is confusing and deceptive, where oppression is government policy, and "slavery is freedom."

Surely, you wouldn't want to become a part of such a world, let alone let it grow under your nose. Orwell's warning about a totalitarian state that aims to destroy democratic space and critical thinking needs to be taken seriously. Any patterns that point in that direction must be called out loud and clear. Platitudes won't suffice. It's high time we called a spade a spade!

Microsoft CEO, Satya Nadella, during the 2017 Build conference said this about the novel, 1984: "*What Orwell prophesied in 1984, where technology was being used to monitor, control, dictate, or what Huxley imagined we may do just by distracting ourselves without any meaning or purpose - neither of these futures is something that we want?'*

2

Totalitarianism, Fiction, and Power of Language in Orwell's 1984

George Orwell intended 1984 to be a political satire where he could share his *"disillusionment with the present as well as his fear of the future."*[9] For him, literature offered a secure haven to reflect on his views about his political era, a feeling that contemporary writers such as Arundhati Roy echo.

According to Roy, *"Only fiction can be true because the truth cannot be told,"*[10] especially when it concerns the politics of the time, which makes speaking about it even more challenging. No wonder, then, that Orwell relied so heavily on fiction to expose the excesses of the politics he witnessed during his time.

---

[9] The Dynamics of Terror in Orwell's "1984" by Malcolm R. Thorp

[10] PEN America Arthur Miller Freedom to Write Lecture - Arundhati Roy

(https://www.theguardian.com/commentisfree/2019/may/13/arundhati-roy-literature-shelter-pen-america)

Through his prescient novels, Nineteen Eighty-Four and Animal Farm, he created a platform to reflect on and criticize the politics of his era. For him, 1984 is *"a fantasy"*[11] steeped in facts:

"This is a political age. War, fascism, concentration camps, rubber truncheons, atomic bombs, etc., are what we daily think about, even when we do not name them openly. We cannot help this. When you are on a sinking ship, your thoughts will be about sinking ships."[12]

In his fiction, Orwell laments the rise of totalitarianism and the degradation of human values. He warns against people's compliance and unquestioning obedience to an authoritarian regime, as this irrational political behavior fuels fascism, which is emboldened by a lack of oversight.

Orwell's experience as a volunteer in the Civil War in Spain allowed him to foresee the genesis of a totalitarian future. The sentiment is echoed by George Bolling (from Orwell's novel, Coming Up for Air) when he says, *"All the things you've got at the back of your mind, the things you're terrified of, the things that you tell yourself are just a nightmare ... There's no escape."*

***

---

[11] "In Front of Your Nose, 1945-1950" The Collected Essays, Journalism and Letters of George Orwell
[12] The Collected Essays, Journalism and Letters of George Orwell

Winston Smith, the protagonist of Orwell's 1984, resides in Oceania, a state where the ruling party, Ingsoc, monopolizes social and political discourse, leaving citizens like Winston unable to understand their exploitation and plight. As pointed out by Malcolm R. Thorp in The Dynamics of Terror in Orwell's 1984, Winston undergoes a *"mid-life identity crisis"* as he fails to make sense of the *"reality of power within Oceania."*

This theme is recurring in Orwell's books, including Animal Farm. In this dystopian world, the party encourages adherence to the party line and discourages reliance on sensory experiences through organs like eyes and ears. One is not supposed to lend credibility to their own experiences but instead to what the party wants them to believe. As Orwell wrote in 1984: *"The Party told you to reject the evidence of your eyes and ears."*[13]

"... animals are not aware of the extent of their plight, for the memory of the old days has fled, leaving them with no way to evaluate if they are better or worse off than before the revolution."[14]

Winston attempts to resist and revolt against the all-encompassing Thoughtpolice whose job is to eliminate any unspoken beliefs that contradict the

---

[13] Trump's Orwellian Doublespeak Will Keep Trumpism Alive (https://www.latimes.com/opinion/story/2020-11-22/trumps-orwellian-doublespeak-trumpism)

[14] Thorp, Malcolm R. "The Dynamics of Terror in Orwell's '1984.'" Brigham Young University Studies, vol. 24, no. 1, 1984, pp. 3–17. JSTOR, http://www.jstor.org/stable/43041004. Accessed 27 Apr. 2023.

Party. He believes that the Thoughtpolice cannot penetrate his mind, allowing him to think freely. However, this proves to be detrimental as the Thoughtpolice, who were monitoring him all along, eventually arrest him.

After being held captive in Room 101, Winston comprehends the power dynamics at play in Oceania and ultimately surrenders his mental freedom to Big Brother, resigning himself to live as a mindless puppet. It's interesting to note that the ruling party of Oceania is Ingsoc, short for English socialism. However, Ingsoc doesn't follow any particular ideology and instead operates under the control of a managerial elite, similar to present-day oligarchies. In reality, technocrats, intellectuals, scientists, and politicians exercise power in Oceania.

Winston's job in the Ministry of Truth is to alter or erase any facts that contradict the party's propaganda. The government uses a variety of tactics to maintain control, including hidden microphones, two-way televisions, dictaphones, helicopter patrols, propaganda broadcasts, and Two Minute Hate drills, which are designed to keep the population deceived and completely submissive.

"Truth is not external. Reality exists in the human mind and nowhere else."[15] In other words, the state must take drastic, yet draconian steps to ensure conformity with party propaganda. Free access to information threatens the regime's control, as it may lead people to think freely and rationally.

---

[15] George Orwell, Nineteen Eighty-Four

Totalitarian regimes do not want their subjects to consume information unfiltered by state-sponsored propaganda. Independent-minded individuals without a stake in party ideologies are the most feared by authoritarian despots.

Acting as gatekeepers, the totalitarian regime in Oceania controls which information to feed into the minds of its citizens and which information to block. People subjected to misinformation and disinformation are easier to subjugate and rule over, as their opinions and perceptions are shaped through controlled media, which is crucial for the regime's existence. Additionally, the intellectual efficacy of individuals is rendered useless and ineffective by *"Doublethink."*[16]

Doublethink is a mental state in which an individual is conditioned to accept two contradictory beliefs simultaneously, which is inherently irrational.

"To know and not to know, to be conscious of complete truthfulness while telling carefully constructed lies, to hold simultaneously two opinions which cancelled out, knowing them to be contradictory and believing in both of them, to use logic against logic, to repudiate morality while laying claim to it, to believe that democracy was impossible and that the

---

[16] "The act of simultaneously accepting two mutually contradictory beliefs as correct. Four examples of doublethink used throughout 1984 include the slogans: War is Peace, Freedom is Slavery, Ignorance is Strength, and 2 + 2 = 5." - Center for Arts, George Mason University (https://cfa.gmu.edu/news/2019-10/big-brother-and-other-terms-1984)

Party was the guardian of democracy, to forget whatever it was necessary to forget, then to draw it back into memory again at the moment when it was needed, and then promptly to forget it again, and above all, to apply the same process to the process itself—that was the ultimate subtlety: consciously to induce unconsciousness, and then, once again, to become unconscious of the act of hypnosis you had just performed. Even to understand the word—doublethink—involved the use of doublethink."[17]

With such a strong emphasis on inner conformity in Ingsoc, members are expected to align their thoughts, opinions, and even their most private emotions with the party ideology. Therefore, simply displaying outward conformity is not enough to succeed in such a regime. An ardent party worker is a "Goodthinker" because they do not think for themselves and have no beliefs, thoughts, or opinions outside of what the party propagates. Anxiety, on the other hand, is symptomatic of self-doubt. Questioning or doubting the party's stated principles and actions is likely to land oneself in trouble due to the fear and anxiety associated with self-doubt.

Without the party ideology, individuals in Oceania lack any sense of identity because they have no access to past experiences or future aspirations. The absence of such experiences and aspirations prevents the people of Oceania from perceiving reality from any other perspective but the one dictated by the party. Put simply, "*Who*

---

[17] George Orwell, Nineteen Eighty-Four

controls the past ... controls the future: who controls the present controls the past."[18] As there is no standard template against which to judge their present experiences, members of Ingsoc tend to overlook their party's fallibility and blindly follow the party ideology. Without a baseline to compare to, they fail to recognize the flaws in the party's doctrine and become indoctrinated to believe in the infallibility of the party.

---

[18] George Orwell, Nineteen Eighty-Four

3
UNDERSTANDING THE TERM 'ORWELLIAN'

George Orwell's influence endures through his impactful words such as "thought police," "doublethink," and "newspeak," which remain relevant today. The New York Times reports that no other writer's name is as commonly used as an adjective as "Orwellian," surpassing even terms like "Kafkaesque," "Hemingwayesque," and "Dickensian" combined.[19]

Its meaning is flexible yet precise, fitting to offer *"contradictory strands of meaning"*[20] to describe not only a regime practicing surveillance and thought control but also a person who manipulates language to suit

---

[19] Simpler Terms; If It's 'Orwellian,' It's Probably Not - The New York Times
(https://www.nytimes.com/2003/06/22/weekinreview/simpler-terms-if-it-s-orwellian-it-s-probably-not.html)
[20] Do you Really Know What 'Orwellian' Means? - The Guardian
(https://www.theguardian.com/books/booksblog/2014/nov/11/reading-group-orwellian-1984)

their purposes. In an Orwellian context, language is complicit in perpetuating the tyranny of a totalitarian regime.[21]

To such an extent that even a leader with a clear inclination towards authoritarianism can be considered Orwellian, as can individuals like Winston Smith, staunch Ingsoc loyalist, and even the general public who are overly submissive and conform religiously to the dictates of their political masters.

Similarly, using political language for thought control and non-stop propaganda is Orwellian, and an uncritical audience reduced to being mere puppets are also characterized by Orwellian qualities by being insensitive to their exploitation and predicament.

Describing himself as unimpeachable, as Donald J. Trump did, is not only appalling but also reminiscent of Orwellian doublespeak.[22] Unfortunately, he's not the first leader to exhibit such *"sociopathic and narcissistic behaviors."*[23] Many

---

[21] "Political language . . . is designed to make lies sound truthful and murder respectable, and to give an appearance of solidity to pure wind." - Politics and the English Language

[22] Trump Says He's Unimpeachable Because He's the 'Greatest' 'Most Successful' President - The Daily Beast (https://www.thedailybeast.com/trump-says-hes-unimpeachabl e-because-hes-the-greatest-most-successful-president)

[23] Burkle F. M. (2019). Character Disorders among Autocratic World Leaders and the Impact on Health Security, Human Rights, and Humanitarian Care. Prehospital and disaster medicine, 34(1), 2–7. https://doi.org/10.1017/S1049023X18001280

leaders display such tendencies, which are often rooted in their fear of insecurity and insatiable need for power. In such cases, language is used to obscure and manipulate reality to maintain and consolidate power, rather than to communicate truth.

An audience that does not think critically, as Orwell asserted, is "favorable to political conformity."[24] And the tool that enables this uncritical political conformity is the "manipulation of language." Once swayed into submission through politically motivated propaganda, seemingly innocuous but Orwellian expressions like "steal,"[25] "migrants," "termites,"[26] "jobs and growth," "family values" and "choice" take root and slowly, with willful consent from the audience, spread their tentacles and disguised fangs to destroy what little remains of human values. For example, *a minister who calls migrants termites* in a tirade against them..[27]

---

[24] Politics and the English Language - The Orwell Foundation (https://www.orwellfoundation.com/the-orwell-foundation/orwell/essays-and-other-works/politics-and-the-english-language/)

[25] Do immigrants "steal" jobs from American workers? - Brookings (https://www.brookings.edu/blog/brookings-now/2017/08/24/do-immigrants-steal-jobs-from-american-workers/)

[26] Bangladeshi Migrants are Like Termites: Amit Shah - The Hindu (https://www.thehindu.com/news/national/bangladeshi-migrants-are-like-termites-amit-shah/article25017064.ece)

[27] BJP chief slammed for calling Bangladeshi migrants 'termites' - Al Jazeera (https://www.aljazeera.com/news/2018/9/24/bjp-chief-slammed-for-calling-bangladeshi-migrants-termites)

This type of political language deprives people of their capacity to think critically and "narrows the range of thought."[28] It is characteristic of Orwellianism to alter the definitions of words and affix negative connotations to them to please party ideologues.

Trump's rhetoric about immigrants "taking our jobs … they're taking our manufacturing jobs … they're taking our money"[29] is not supported by the findings of the National Bureau of Economic Research. In fact, the bureau stated that "immigrants appear to create jobs (expand labor demand) more than they take jobs (expand labor supply) in the U.S. economy … account for closer to one-quarter of U.S. patents."[30]

In short, the term "Orwellian" has multiple and often contradictory meanings that can apply to both the oppressor and the oppressed. However, for a straightforward explanation of the term, the Cambridge Dictionary offers the following definition:

" … *used to describe a political system in which the government tries to control every part of people's lives, similar*

---

[28] 1984 Quotes, Mind Control - SparkNotes
(https://www.sparknotes.com/lit/1984/quotes/theme/mind-control/)

[29] AP Fact Check: Trump Plays on Immigration Myths - PBS Newshour
(https://www.pbs.org/newshour/politics/ap-fact-check-trump-plays-on-immigration-myths)

[30] Immigration and Entrepreneurship in the United States
(http://conference.nber.org/conf_papers/f142369.pdf)

to that described in the novel "Nineteen Eighty-Four", by George Orwell."[31]

Wikipedia defines Orwellian as "an adjective describing a situation, idea, or societal condition that George Orwell identified as being destructive to the welfare of a free and open society. It denotes an attitude and a brutal policy of draconian control by propaganda, surveillance, disinformation, denial of truth (doublethink), and manipulation of the past … practised by modern repressive governments."[32]

It is important to recognize that the term Orwellian encompasses a range of meanings, including the "manipulative use of language, mass surveillance, and intrusive government."[33] Furthermore, it is worth noting that even individuals who are guilty of disliking others' ideas on baseless grounds can be accused of bearing Orwellian tendencies.

Orwell's warnings about the dangers of totalitarianism extend beyond non-democratic governments, as even democracies can become Orwellian if complacency sets in. He believed that the proliferation of self-serving ideologies and opinions of authoritarian leaders, at the expense of the public good, could lead to a decay of society.

---

[31] Meaning of Orwellian in English - Cambridge Dictionary
(https://dictionary.cambridge.org/dictionary/english/orwellian)
[32] Orwellian - Wikipedia
(https://en.wikipedia.org/wiki/Orwellian)
[33] What "Orwellian" really means - Noah Tavlin - TEDEd
(https://ed.ted.com/lessons/what-orwellian-really-means-noah-tavlin#digdeeper)

One of the most concerning things for Orwell was the use of euphemisms by political leaders to hide truth and avoid promoting critical thinking. This abuse of language is not only present in politics, but also in advertising and political campaigns, which can sway public support at the expense of their own well-being.

4
EXAMINING TRUMP'S USE OF LANGUAGE THROUGH AN ORWELLIAN LENS

Trump is known for his candidness and his tendency to resort to Orwellian doublespeak. He has lied and took refuge in his lies on multiple occasions, such as when he inflated the size of his inauguration crowd to unimaginable proportions. He also falsely believed that the coronavirus would go away miraculously, and his polarizing rhetoric has further divided society along racial lines. Additionally, he has propagated the unfounded conspiracy theory of "election fraud."[34]

Trump's Orwellian rhetoric is too simplistic, unconvincing, and lack imagination. Many Americans have turned to Orwell's novel to make

---

[34] Dana Milbank, In Trump's Mind, it's Always 'Really Sunny.' And that's Terrifying. - The Washington Post (https://www.washingtonpost.com/opinions/in-trumps-mind-its-always-really-sunny-and-thats-terrifying/2017/01/27/ff0a6278-e499-11e6-a547-5fb9411d332c_story.html)

sense of the Trump administration's tactics, resulting in a *9,500 percent increase in sales*.[35] However, the label of "Orwellian" is not limited to one political party; both liberals and conservatives have used it to describe their opponents. Trump himself has decried the ban of his father from Twitter as evidence that "we are living Orwell's 1984," accusing the social media giant of censoring public speech.

Trump seems to have a connection with George Orwell's "1984," as it often follows him wherever he goes and whatever he says. In Trump's presidency, it's easier to spot remnants of Orwellian language.

During a Kansas City convention, he made the statement, *"What you're seeing and what you're reading is not what's happening,"*[36] which people quickly compared to a similar sentiment expressed in 1984: *"The party told you to reject the evidence of your eyes and ears. It was their final, most essential command."*[37]

Trump was aware that his statements were false, but he sought to convince people to believe in him regardless of the evidence. If his decision to impose

---

[35] The Word "Orwellian" Has Lost All Meaning - Vox (https://www.vox.com/culture/22233197/orwellian-definition-george-orwell-1984-politics-english-language-josh-hawley-donald-trump-jr)

[36] 'What You're Seeing... Is Not What's Happening.' People Are Comparing This Trump Quote to George Orwell - Time (https://time.com/5347737/trump-quote-george-orwell-vfw-speech/)

[37] George Orwell, Nineteen Eighty-Four

tariffs on China had been successful, he would not have needed to introduce a *$12 billion aid package to support farmers adversely affected by the policy.*[38]

Following his inaugural speech, Trump quickly began to create a narrative of fantasy and self-delusion. He claimed to have drawn a crowd of 250,000 people for his inaugural address and insisted that the rain had stopped and the sun had come out during his speech, only to start pouring again after he left.[39]

"God looked down and he said, we're not going to let it rain on your speech … The first line, I got hit by a couple of drops … But the truth is that it stopped immediately … And then it became really sunny. And then I walked off and it poured right after I left."

This is a clear example of the descent into denial of reality that Orwell warned against in 1984. Columnist Dana Milbank has likened it to "Trump declaring black is white or day is night," which is reminiscent of Orwellian doublespeak that accepts contrary beliefs as correct, such as "Ignorance is Strength" and "Freedom is Slavery," which just undermines the meaning of words.

Trump's assertion that it stopped raining and became sunny during his inaugural speech is a clear departure from reality. Milbank, who was present at

---

[38] Trump Administration Plans $12 Billion In Farm Aid To Offset Tariffs - NPR
(https://www.npr.org/2018/07/24/631953880/trump-administration-to-provide-farmers-12-billion-to-offset-tariffs)
[39] Trump CIA Speech Transcript - CBS News
(https://www.cbsnews.com/news/trump-cia-speech-transcript/)

the inauguration, stated that he couldn't recall "*a single ray of sunshine, before, during or after the speech.*"[40]

Authoritarian leaders across ages and across the world have demonstrated an uncanny ability to indulge in self-delusion and a disconnection from reality, which is truly bewildering. As the boundaries between truth and lies become blurred, the propensity to lie spirals out of control, with those in power using state machinery and controlled media to construct alternate realities.

Too often, public officials are coerced into agreeing with their leaders' quixotic fantasies.[41] The driving force behind their falsehoods is often the belief that even if something isn't true, it "at least ought to be true."[42]

---

[40] Dana Milbank, In Trump's Mind, it's Always 'Really Sunny.' And that's Terrifying. - The Washington Post (https://www.washingtonpost.com/opinions/in-trumps-mind-its-always-really-sunny-and-thats-terrifying/2017/01/27/ff0a6278-e499-11e6-a547-5fb9411d332c_story.html)

[41] Tump Pressured Park Service to Find Proof for his Claims About Inauguration Crowd - The Washington Post (https://www.washingtonpost.com/politics/trump-pressured-park-service-to-back-up-his-claims-about-inauguration-crowd/2017/01/26/12a38cb8-e3fc-11e6-ba11-63c4b4fb5a63_story.html)

[42] Tony Schwartz, Donald Trump's Ghostwriter Tells All, The New Yorker (https://www.newyorker.com/magazine/2016/07/25/donald-trumps-ghostwriter-tells-all)

5

TRUMP'S POLITICAL LANGUAGE AND CRITICAL THINKING

According to the Washington Post's Fact Checker, "President Trump made over 30,573 false or misleading claims"[43] during his time in office. His deliberate attempt to blur the line between fact and fiction is concerning, as it undermines the importance of objective truth and critical thinking. Despite facing criticism and pushback, Trump appears unwilling to concede to factual reality.

This may be due to his narcissistic tendencies, which prioritize his own beliefs and opinions over evidence and reason. In this way, Trump's worldview is disconnected from that of the general public, leading to a dangerous fragmentation of reality.

If the aim is to cause discord and confusion

---

[43] In Four Years, President Trump Made 30,573 False or Misleading Claims, Fact Checker - The Washington Post (https://www.washingtonpost.com/graphics/politics/trump-clai ms-database/)

where there should be understanding, then *"slippery (or misleading) political language"*[44] is an effective tool. Authoritarianism is the result of both political cunning and distorted language.

In George Orwell's dystopian novel 1984, language and oppression are intimately linked in a totalitarian state. Critical thinking is the enemy of oppressive ideology, which is why it is so reviled and suppressed. Since one cannot force the elimination of critical thoughts buried deep within the mind, the best and only weapon available to crush critical thinking is through the manipulation of language.

Autocratic rulers are not bound by the constraints of factual language. Their inclination towards contradictions is evident in the way they conduct public affairs, with a clear divide between their words and actions. For example, Trump claimed to be the "No. 1 environmental president"[45] despite withdrawing from the Paris Agreement.[46]

---

[44] From Doublespeak to Alternative Facts: How Trump Made a Mess of the Language - Grist
(https://grist.org/politics/from-doublespeak-to-alternative-facts-how-trump-made-a-mess-of-the-language/)
[45] Trump Declares Himself "the No. 1 Environmental President" - Vanity Fair
(https://www.vanityfair.com/news/2020/09/donald-trump-environment-roosevelt)
[46] Climate change: US Formally Withdraws From Paris Agreement - BBC
(https://www.bbc.com/news/science-environment-54797743)

The use of euphemisms such as "rising natural hazard risk"[47] and "overheating planet" in official language is a deliberate attempt to avoid "mentioning the words climate change"[48] and manufacture doubt about the "man-made environmental crisis."[49]

The Trump administration's lack of clarity on its plans for environmental action, combined with vague terms like "resilience" and "sustainability," downplayed the severity of the crisis. While Trump talks of being "resilient and adapt to a changing future," farmers suffer from devastating floods and droughts.

Trump relies heavily on slippery, euphemistic language to shape his own version of reality. He calls his lies 'real' and cloaks them in the "appearance of solidity"[50] through political

---

[47] A Guide To Talking About Climate Change Like A Trump Official - Grist (https://grist.org/article/cant-bring-yourself-to-say-climate-change-try-these-trump-ready-phrases-instead/)

[48] Trump Applies Obama-Era Flood Aid Rules He Axed Six Months Ago - Bloomberg (https://www.bloomberg.com/news/articles/2018-02-07/trump-applies-obama-era-flood-aid-rules-it-axed-six-months-ago?leadSource=uverify%20wall)

[49] A Brief Overview Of Climate Denialism In The U.S., Changing The Digital Climate, How Climate Change Web Content is Being Censored Under the Trump Administration - Environment Data & Governance Initiative (https://envirodatagov.org/wp-content/uploads/2018/01/Part-3-Changing-the-Digital-Climate.pdf)

[50] George Orwell, Politics and the English Language

language. He expects others to adopt his language in order to see the world through his distorted lens.

This requires abandoning "concrete language"[51]and critical thinking in favor of nonsensical language and reality that does not truly exist. As Orwell notes, it is crucial to remain "tethered to reality" by using "your eyes"[52] to see what is actually happening, rather than relying solely on language to shape your understanding of the world.

Trump operates in the opposite direction, telling *"deliberate lies while genuinely believing in them,"*[53]a phenomenon Orwell referred to as doublethink. This assault on reality is particularly unnerving in an era where the line between real and unreal is rapidly blurring, thanks to the rise of *deepfake*[54] and other

---

(https://www.orwellfoundation.com/the-orwell-foundation/orwell/essays-and-other-works/politics-and-the-english-language/)

[51] Kate Yoder (Staff Writer at Grist): "What George Orwell Can Teach Us About Trump's Environmental Lies." (https://grist.org/politics/from-doublespeak-to-alternative-facts-how-trump-made-a-mess-of-the-language/)

[52] Jean Seaton (Director of the Orwell Foundation): "Here's the thing about Orwell. He's in favor of using your eyes, seeing where you live, being tethered to reality as far as you could be."

[53] Peter C. Herman, Orwell's "1984" and Trump's Presidency - Areo Magazine (https://areomagazine.com/2020/11/30/orwells-1984-and-trumps-presidency/)

[54] Facing Reality? Law Enforcement And The Challenge Of Deepfakes - Europol (https://www.europol.europa.eu/publications-events/publications/facing-reality-law-enforcement-and-challenge-of-deepfakes)

Artificial Intelligence tools that can be used for nefarious purposes like spreading disinformation and misinformation. This trend could give rise to absolute skepticism, where people even question established scientific norms.

One of the primary tactics employed by autocratic leaders like Trump is the deliberate distortion of language to limit vocabulary, which, as Peter C. Herman notes, "narrow[s] the range of thought."[55]

Why bother with long press conferences when a tweet can convey the same message? In both Orwell's 1984 and Trump's speeches, a preference for limited vocabulary is evident. The aim of this tactic is to stifle critical thinking and limit independent thought, a hallmark of all fascist regimes modeled after Orwell's dystopian world.

---

[55] Peter C. Herman, Orwell's "1984" and Trump's Presidency: "The whole point of Newspeak," says Symes, the Party philologist who is working on the 11th edition of the Newspeak dictionary, "is to narrow the range of thought."

6

POWER, PRIVILEGE, AND ENTERPRISE: THE HALLMARKS OF A TOTALITARIAN REGIME

As the fear of public outcry diminishes, there are few barriers preventing a regime from transforming into a private enterprise with an elected head of state at its helm. As regimes install their cronies to head independent institutions, the once-clear separation between various pillars of the state—legislative, executive, judiciary, and media—erodes, leading to an oligarchic setup.

In this setup, a select few from the business, bureaucratic, and political establishment have unhindered access to state coffers, resources, militias, and other state apparatuses to wield power and privilege.

Within such an enterprise, there is a clear discrepancy between what the people want and what the regime imposes on them. To garner popular support, regimes manipulate reality to persuade their audience.

While the people yearn for democracy, accountability, and transparency in governance, fascist powers sow seeds of discord and disharmony and often resort to military adventurism to rally the people under the banner of nationalism.

Manipulating nationalism is a common tactic used by totalitarian regimes to distract people from their legitimate demands for freedom, democracy, and accountability. Meanwhile, a well-oiled state machinery takes advantage of the lack of transparency to funnel public funds into private pockets, often under the guise of "economic development" or "national security." Those who remain loyal to the regime are rewarded with economic benefits, power, and prestige, while those who deviate from the official line are neutralized. The result is an oligarchic setup where a few elites control the state apparatus and its resources, while the masses are left to fend for themselves without access to basic amenities.

***

Orwell's 1984 exemplifies this same phenomenon. In the novel, food is rationed and basic commodities such as razor blades are scarce. Only members of the Inner Party, who form the privileged elite of Oceanic society, have the authority to turn off the ubiquitous telescreen.

O'Brien,[56] an Inner Party member, admits to Winston Smith that they have this privilege."[57] Similarly, Julia, a key character in the novel who possesses knowledge beyond Winston's, remarks that "There's nothing those swine don't have, nothing."[58] Although ration cuts are a regular occurrence in 1984, Inner Party members are shielded from the harsh reality of food shortages due to their elevated status.

***

Modern oligarchies are no different. The privileges of a select few have turned them blind to the suffering of millions. In Trump's America, his close associates can violate the Hatch Act[59] with impunity. Ryan Zinke, who served as the interior secretary in the Trump administration, and Kellyanne Conway have not only violated the act

---

[56] O'Brien, 1984 Characters, SparkNotes (https://www.sparknotes.com/lit/1984/character/obrien/)

[57] Peter C. Herman, Rules Don't Apply at the Top, Orwell's "1984" and Trump's Presidency - Areo Magazine (https://areomagazine.com/2020/11/30/orwells-1984-and-trumps-presidency/)

[58] George Orwell, Nineteen Eighty-Four

[59] "The Hatch Act, a federal law passed in 1939, limits certain political activities of federal employees … to protect federal employees from political coercion in the workplace, and to ensure that federal employees are advanced based on merit and not based on political affiliation." - Hatch Act Overview, U.S. Office of Special Counsel (https://osc.gov/Services/Pages/HatchAct.aspx)

but have also done so unapologetically.[60]

Intelligence officials denied security clearance to Jared Kushner, Trump's son-in-law, but Trump coerced officials into granting him clearance. Despite his initial denial of involvement, an internal memo by John F. Kelly, the White House chief of staff, revealed that Trump "ordered" top-secret clearance to be given to Kushner, despite clear objections from intelligence officials and White House counsel Donald F. McGahn II.[61]

This blurs *"the lines of family, nation and business,"*[62] as described by Noah Bierman and Chris Megerian in a Los Angeles Times story, whereby officeholders pursue family and business interests while on national duty. Ivanka Trump's official role as an advisor to the president granted her access to foreign leaders and business heads.

It is no surprise, then, that Ivanka was able to

---

[60] The Energy 202: Federal Investigators Concluded Ryan Zinke's MAGA Socks Violated Law - The Washinton Post (https://www.washingtonpost.com/news/powerpost/paloma/the-energy-202/2019/06/06/the-energy-202-federal-investigators-concluded-ryan-zinke-s-maga-socks-violated-law/5cf80667a7a0a46b92a3ffff/)

[61] Trump Ordered Officials to Give Jared Kushner a Security Clearance - The New York Times (https://www.nytimes.com/2019/02/28/us/politics/jared-kushner-security-clearance.html)

[62] Noah Bierman and Chris Megerian, Trump's Children Take In Millions Overseas As President Slams Biden's Son - Los Angeles Times (https://www.latimes.com/politics/story/2019-10-10/trumps-adult-children-do-business-overseas-as-president-slams-biden)

secure a "dozen Chinese trademarks," and three trademark approvals immediately after her dinner with Chinese President Xi Jinping in April 2017, covering products such as "jewellery, handbags and spa services."

The Trump family has denied any allegations of impropriety, but as Robert Maguire notes, there may be more to the story, *"especially when private projects depend on foreign governments that are looking to bolster ties with Washington."*[63]

According to Maguire, profiting from the presidency is a serious accusation that cannot be easily dismissed with a simple denial:

"With President Trump, we know his two adult sons are going around the country and the world to make money for a company that President Trump himself personally profits from, that he also personally promotes using the White House."[64]

***

The reality that power yields privilege, as it was for George Orwell, continues to be true even today.

---

[63] Those Foreign Business Ties? The Trump Sons Have Plenty Too - The New York Times (https://www.nytimes.com/2019/10/11/us/politics/donald-trump-jr-eric-trump-business.html)

[64] Noah Bierman and Chris Megerian, Trump's Children Take In Millions Overseas As President Slams Biden's Son - Los Angeles Times (https://www.latimes.com/politics/story/2019-10-10/trumps-adult-children-do-business-overseas-as-president-slams-biden)

Leaders who wield more power often consider themselves above the law. Those close to such leaders take advantage of privileged positions to get away with any breach of law and order.

This is the case in Modi's India also, where serious offenders commit heinous crimes with an air of impunity and are even garlanded by sitting ministers.[65] When crime is institutionalized, as racism was in South Africa and still is to some extent in the United States and elsewhere, it gives rise to new gangs under the direct patronage of the state who use them as pawns to eliminate political rivals or win loyalties.

Putin's Russia employs organized crime and disinformation as an *asymmetric arsenal*[66] in the war against democracy and the rule of law, similar to how *cow vigilantism is used in India.*[67] Putin uses these tactics to win the loyalty of opponents, much like what happens in Orwell's 1984.

---

[65] Zeba Warsi, Outrage in India as 11 Men Convicted of Rape and Murders in Gujarat Violence Walk Free - PBS Newshour (https://www.pbs.org/newshour/world/ghost-of-the-2002-gujarat-violence-haunts-india-again-as-11-men-convicted-of-rape-and-murders-walk-free)

[66] Putin's Asymmetric Assault On Democracy In Russia And Europe: Implications For U.S. National Security - From the U.S. Government Publishing Office (https://www.govinfo.gov/content/pkg/CPRT-115SPRT28110/html/CPRT-115SPRT28110.htm)

[67] India: Vigilante 'Cow Protection' Groups Attack Minorities - Human Rights Watch (https://www.hrw.org/news/2019/02/19/india-vigilante-cow-protection-groups-attack-minorities)

In the novel, Winston Smith is subjected to severe political repression and exposed to daily propaganda from O'Brien, which transforms him from a revolutionary to a staunch loyalist of Big Brother.

Across countries like in Putin's Russia, Modi's India, Trump's America, Pakistan's military establishment, and elsewhere, political allies are given significant social, political, and economic power. They enjoy extreme wealth, often beyond their known means, and their financial transactions are difficult to trace. This lack of transparency creates suspicions of corruption and cronyism.

War is a constant presence in the world of 1984's Oceania.[68] Orwell believed that oppressive regimes require external aggression to justify their repressive policies, divert attention from domestic issues, and silence dissent. War stokes fear in the populace, who turn to the state for protection, and the state demands loyalty and obedience in exchange.

"Oceania has always been at war with Eastasia. Since the beginning of your life, since the beginning of the Party, since the beginning of history, the war has continued without a break, always the same war."[69]

Like Big Brother, Russian President Vladimir

---

[68] Oceania in 1984 by George Orwell - Overview
(https://study.com/academy/lesson/oceania-in-1984.html)
[69] George Orwell, Nineteen Eighty-Four
(https://www.abhaf.org/assets/books/html/1984/169.html#)

Putin seems to use "war to achieve internal political objectives."[70] Putin is supported by Russian oligarchs who know their economic interests lie in supporting the government enterprise, rather than raising their voice against state surveillance and harassment of human rights activists and journalists. These oligarchs have already amassed an estimated $24 billion in illicit money through illegal means.[71]

The opposition leaders are greatly concerned by the fact that Oligarchs and crony capitalists use their wealth to influence television and newspaper owners to produce biased content that portrays their authoritarian leader in the best possible light.[72] At the same time, a smear campaign is often launched to discredit political opponents and sway public opinion in their favor.

It is common for powerful leaders like Putin to appoint their allies and cronies to key positions in the judiciary, bureaucracy, military, and state-run

---

[70] Putin's Asymmetric Assault On Democracy In Russia And Europe: Implications For U.S. National Security - From the U.S. Government Publishing Office (https://www.govinfo.gov/content/pkg/CPRT-115SPRT28110/html/CPRT-115SPRT28110.htm)

[71] Putin And The Proxies - Organized Crime and Reporting Project (https://www.occrp.org/en/putinandtheproxies/#stories)

[72] How Putin Conquered Russia's Oligarchy - NPR (https://www.npr.org/sections/money/2022/03/29/1088886554/how-putin-conquered-russias-oligarchy)

companies. These individuals often act as a façade to conceal their master's illicit activities.

According to economist Stanislav Markus of the University of South Carolina, Putin is the ultimate beneficiary of the extra money charged by state-run companies like Gazprom for gas to the state:

"That's what makes Vladimir Putin one of the wealthiest people on the planet. Nobody knows exactly how wealthy, but that's one of the key processes."[73]

Where do the common people stand in all of this? What do they want? What is it that people want but leaders like Putin prefer to withhold?

The Carnegie Endowment for International Peace asked the same question to ordinary Russians and their answers, despite Putin's state-sponsored capitalism and watered-down authoritarianism, came out all too familiar: *"focus on ordinary people,"* *"listen to the people,"* and *"take their needs to heart."*[74] Across the political spectrum, despite ideological differences, ordinary people across the board wanted more democracy, freedom, and accountability.

It is evident that those who hold power in a

---

[73] Of Oligarchs and Silovarchs - NPR, The Indicator (https://www.npr.org/2022/03/15/1086740674/of-oligarchs-and-silovarchs)

[74] How Proponents and Opponents of Political Change See Russia's Future - Carnegie Endowment for International Peace (https://carnegieendowment.org/2021/01/14/how-proponents-and-opponents-of-political-change-see-russia-s-future-pub-8360 Z)

political system are the ones who benefit from it. It is ironic that people have to plead for things they want from a political system that exercises power only on their behalf but cannot change it in the first place. This highlights the degree to which political systems have been hijacked by unseen forces that are beyond the control of ordinary people.

These forces are above the rule of law and hold more weight than the collective votes of all eligible voters. Politics, in the words of John Dewey, is "the shadow cast by business over society."[75] To put it more bluntly, Thomas Ferguson, Paul Jorgensen, and Jie Chen argue that *"We live in a money-driven political system."*[76]

Not all money that enters politics is transparent; much of it is *"dark money flowing in from undisclosed donors."*[77] According to Noam Chomsky, *"Elections are moments when groups of investors coalesce and invest to control the state."*[78] So all in all, there is a strong

---

[75] Money Determines U.S. President
(https://chomsky.info/20041011/)
[76] How Money Drives US Congressional Elections - Institute for New Economic Thinking
(https://www.ineteconomics.org/uploads/papers/WP_48_Fergu son_et_al.pdf)
[77] Maggie Koerth, How Money Affects Elections - FiveThirtyEight CBS News
(https://fivethirtyeight.com/features/money-and-elections-a-co mplicated-love-story/)
[78] Noam Chomsky: "What Next? The Elections, the Economy, and the World" - Democracy Now
(https://www.democracynow.org/2008/11/24/noam_chomsky_ what_next_the_elections)

correlation between corporate spending and election outcomes. The extent of this relationship can be disputed.

For businesses, investing in a political setup is a more profitable path of earning quick profits without engaging in productive activity.[79] In such cases, governments are caught between the wishes of the people and the pressure from corporations for more concessions, often at the expense of ordinary people's well-being. Unfortunately, governments tend to side with corporations, abandoning their promises to the people as soon as they assume office.

This leads us to the conclusion that power and money are intertwined. Anyone with one or both can influence how the government operates from within. Once granted entry into the autocratic leader's private enterprise, pulling the strings from behind becomes even easier.

***

It is even more concerning that corruption is more rampant in poor countries.[80] These fragile economies have even weaker law and order situations, making it easier for government officials

---

[79] Holcombe, R. G. (2013). Crony Capitalism: By-Product of Big Government. The Independent Review, 17(4), 541-559. https://doi.org/10.2307/24563134

[80] Jonathan Macey, The Rise Of Crony Capitalism, Hoover Institution (https://www.hoover.org/research/rise-crony-capitalism)

and business leaders to get away with corrupt practices. When power is at stake, rooting out corruption is often put on the back burner.

This essentially means that going after party members actively involved in corruption may result in them jumping ship just in time to join the opposition camp and bring down the government.

The ruling party often uses corruption as a tool to weaken the opposition. Politicians who have incriminating charges against them are identified and probed by party-controlled agencies. In most cases, the motive is not to bring them to justice but to coerce them into shifting loyalties. If they want the investigation to be halted, they are asked to switch sides.[81]

The antidote to this chaos is a robust and independent judiciary, but even this has lately come under fire. *"We are now seeing increasing and worrying attempts by the executive and legislative to use their leverage to influence and instruct the judiciary and undermine judicial independence."*[82]

Although Israel stands out, where civilians and military personnel have taken to the streets to protest legal reforms that aim to *"weaken the judicial*

---

[81] There Are Significant Exceptions to BJP's 'Tough Stance' Against Corruption - The Wire (https://thewire.in/politics/bjp-corruption-central-agencies-lalu-aap)

[82] Commissioner for Human Rights, The Independence Of Judges And The Judiciary Under Threat - Council of Europe Portal (https://www.coe.int/en/web/commissioner/-/the-independence-of-judges-and-the-judiciary-under-threat)

system,"[83] not many countries have fought as vigorously for a strong judiciary.

Diego García-Sayán, United Nations Special Rapporteur on the Independence of Judges and Lawyers, has identified two principal effects of corruption:[84]

a) *"Corruption deprives societies of important resources that could be used for basic needs, such as public health, education, infrastructure, or security."*

b) *"Corruption has direct damaging consequences in general on the functioning of state institutions, and in particular on the administration of justice."*

If we want to bridge the income disparity and curb government corruption, ensuring judicial oversight for checks and balances on the executive and legislative branches is a prerequisite. This alone can be immensely valuable for a functioning democracy.

***

The rise of *popular nationalism* across a wide variety of countries has infused new life into *crony capitalism*. In fact, the rise of crony capitalism and totalitarianism has been so swift and intertwined

---

[83] Israel Judicial Reform: Why is There a Crisis? - BBC (https://www.bbc.com/news/world-middle-east-65086871)

[84] Diego García-Sayán, Corruption, Human Rights, and Judicial Independence - (https://www.unodc.org/dohadeclaration/en/news/2018/04/corruption--human-rights--and-judicial-independence.html)

that it's hard to see them apart. What drives the rise of totalitarian and populist leaders is *fear and hysteria peddled through 24x7 news channels*, on the one hand, and corporate financing on the other.[85]

The neoliberal agenda involves a deliberate investment in political capital, aimed at *"engineering a redistribution of income and assets in favour of finance capital and big business."*[86] In India, this has been exemplified by Gautam Adani's meteoric rise, which Rahul Gandhi, an Indian politician, alleges was made possible through the blessings of Indian Prime Minister Narendra Modi.[87]

Adani has *"amassed a paper fortune of over U.S. $120 billion, with over $100 billion of that coming in the past 3 years."*[88] His business empire spans multiple sectors, including ports, mines, airports, data centers, power generation, and power transmission, and it is difficult to imagine that he could have

---

[85] Aijaz Ahmad, The State is Taken Over from Within, Frontline (https://frontline.thehindu.com/cover-story/the-state-is-taken-over-from-within/article28617258.ece)

[86] C.P. Chandrasekhar, Indian Neoliberalism: A Toxic Gift from Global Finance - Frontline (https://frontline.thehindu.com/cover-story/indian-neoliberalism-economic-reforms-at-30-a-toxic-gift-from-global-finance/article36290562.ece)

[87] India's Rahul Gandhi Accuses PM Modi of Favoring Adani Group - AP News (https://apnews.com/article/india-gandhi-modi-adani-89e037a70af49cec743592341d20cea5)

[88] Adani Group: How The World's 3rd Richest Man Is Pulling The Largest Con In Corporate History - Hindenburg Research (https://hindenburgresearch.com/adani/)

achieved such dominance without some rules being bent in his favor.[89]

What provides fuel and a strong foundation for divisive right-wing policies that appeal to the masses is their exploitation of the fear of inequality: *"the majority middle, the white worker, slipping steadily into the ranks of the historically disadvantaged—the minorities, the immigrants."*[90]

This means that trade and market-driven inequality, exacerbated by the rise of automation and technology, is given a communal spin, whether in Trump's America or Modi's India. That fear is translated into *anti-immigration rhetoric in America*[91] and *anti-minority discourse in India.*[92] As Raghuram Rajan, the former governor of the Reserve Bank of India, has stated:

---

[89] Explainer: Why Rahul Gandhi Accused Modi Government Of Bending Rules To Hand Over Airports To Adani - Scroll.in (https://scroll.in/article/1043531/explained-why-rahul-gandhi-accused-modi-government-of-bending-rules-to-hand-over-airports-to-adani)

[90] Raghuram Rajan: Populist Nationalism Is "the First Step Toward Crony Capitalism" - ProMarket (https://www.promarket.org/2017/08/30/raghuram-rajan-populist-outcry-cry-help/)

[91] Trump's Anti-Immigrant Rhetoric Was Never About Legality — It Was About Our Brown Skin - Time (https://time.com/5645501/trump-anti-immigration-rhetoric-racism/)

[92] How Hindu Supremacists are Tearing India Apart - The Guardian (https://www.theguardian.com/world/2020/feb/20/hindu-supremacists-nationalism-tearing-india-apart-modi-bjp-rss-jnu-attacks)

"The populist-nationalist is saying 'I am going to recreate community for you—not your broken down community, beset by drugs and divorce, but a national community based on patriotism, based on people like you. 'People like you' is often the majority group, the majority colour, the majority origin."

***

Despite the exploitation of people in the name of nationalism, public intellectuals who attempt to raise awareness are discredited as foreign agents, liberal elites, or anti-nationals due to the deep state control over the media. They use hard facts and rational arguments to enlighten the public, but the media manipulation is so effective that many people don't react or dismiss them as unpatriotic.

This not only tears apart the social fabric but also paves the way for identity politics and crony capitalism. It leads to the looting and plundering of national resources and utilities becoming the norm under such a regime, along with large-scale privatization of the public sector.

On top of that, in the words of Sitaram Yechury, there are *"ruthless attacks on people's democratic rights, civil liberties and human rights; treating all dissent as anti-national, indiscriminately arresting people under draconian laws like UAPA [Unlawful Activities (Prevention) Act]/sedition—a process that undermines the Constitution and its guarantees to the people."*[93]

---

[93] 'A Corporate-Communal Nexus has Emerged': Sitaram Yechury

Moreover, the lack of public reaction in the face of such atrocities can also be attributed to hyperconsumerism and rugged individualism that have dealt a fatal blow to social and political activism over the years.

- Frontline
(https://frontline.thehindu.com/cover-story/interview-sitaram-yechury-neoliberalism-economic-reforms-at-30-a-corporate-communal-nexus-has-emerged/article36288863.ece)

7

THE DOWNFALL OF SOCIAL AND POLITICAL ACTIVISM IN THE AGE OF HYPERCONSUMERISM AND INDIVIDUALISM

The enterprise is deeply entrenched. At the lower end are the taxpaying middle class, who enjoy limited financial stability that should have been sufficient to last them a lifetime. However, *hyperconsumerism*[94] cuts it short and makes them part of the enterprise anyway.

As a result, their silence on state oppression is understandable but not excusable. As a privileged class, they have chosen to maintain the status quo rather than challenge it. Speaking out against exploitation means jeopardizing their position

---

[94] "Hyperconsumerism is the consumption of goods beyond one's necessities and the associated significant pressure to consume those goods, exerted by social media and other outlets as those goods are perceived to shape one's identity." Hyperconsumerism - Wikipedia
(https://en.wikipedia.org/wiki/Hyperconsumerism)

within the larger scheme of the enterprise.

Their economic prosperity is linked to the enterprise, regardless of its corruption, inhumanity, or injustice. Their silence ensures two things: they continue to receive the watered-down benefits of the enterprise, and trouble never comes their way. It's a bargain they remain loyal to.

In other words, their *"social relations are increasingly commercialized … and cede civil liberties in the hope of achieving more favorable living conditions."*[95] As more people are subjected to *state oppression* on unfounded grounds, there is less for them to care about.

Most tax systems tend to burden the middle class while leaving the ultra-rich untouched. In the United States, for example, the White House economists point out that *"When a middle class American earns a dollar of wages, that dollar is taxed immediately. But when a billionaire makes a dollar because their stocks increase in value, that dollar is taxed at a preferred rate—if it's ever taxed at all."*[96]

---

[95] Consumption Practices and Middle-Class Consciousness among Socially Aware Shoppers in Atlanta - Georgia State University (https://scholarworks.gsu.edu/cgi/viewcontent.cgi?referer=&httpsredir=1&article=1012&context=anthro_theses)

[96] New OMB-CEA Report: Billionaires Pay an Average Federal Individual Income Tax Rate of Just 8.2% - White House Blog (https://www.whitehouse.gov/omb/briefing-room/2021/09/23/new-omb-cea-report-billionaires-pay-an-average-federal-individual-income-tax-rate-of-just-8-2/)

As a result, *the 400 wealthiest Americans pay lower tax rates than many ordinary Americans.*[97] For instance, while a median American household earning $70,000 pays 14% in federal taxes, the richest 25 Americans, whose worth rose to a collective $401 billion from 2014 to 2018, paid only $13.6 billion in federal income taxes for the same period, which is a tax rate of just 3.4%.[98]

The middle class often resents the oppressed and downtrodden, believing that they are already bearing a heavy economic burden through taxation and cannot fight their socio-political battles for them. Additionally, average middle-class families face immense socio-cultural pressure to climb the socioeconomic ladder, achieving a lifestyle that is comparably luxurious to the upper class.[99]

This race for refinement has given birth to a culture of rugged individualism that has blinded the middle class to repressive political agendas. With an "everyone for themselves" attitude, political othering has become difficult to curtail. As a result,

---

[97] The Forbes 400 Pay Lower Tax Rates Than Many Ordinary Americans - Center for American Progress (https://www.americanprogress.org/article/forbes-400-pay-lower-tax-rates-many-ordinary-americans/)

[98] The Secret IRS Files: Trove of Never-Before-Seen Records Reveal How the Wealthiest Avoid Income Tax - ProPublica (https://www.propublica.org/article/the-secret-irs-files-trove-of-never-before-seen-records-reveal-how-the-wealthiest-avoid-income-tax)

[99] Lois Tyson, Marxist Criticism, Critical Theory Today, Routledge

xenophobia is on the rise, human rights violations have skyrocketed, and majoritarianism has reduced minorities to second-class citizens.[100] All of this is happening while the political space for dissent has shrunk and speaking up invites the wrath of the state.

***

The combination of rugged individualism and hyperconsumerism has dealt a significant blow to social activism that relies on mass participation to bring about substantial socio-political change. The pursuit of perpetual economic prosperity has led ordinary people to be apathetic towards supporting social activism, which was once a collective effort to transform the social order. As Umair Muhammad argues:

"Individualism should imply uniqueness, difference, originality among individuals; that is to say, it should imply individuality. Oddly enough, the age of individualism is also the age of conformity."[101]

Consumerism, on the other hand, has led to the mass production of goods. There is pressure on the

---

[100] Turning Minority Into "2nd Class Citizens" Will Divide India: R Rajan - NDTV (https://www.ndtv.com/india-news/turning-minority-into-2nd-class-citizens-will-divide-india-raghuram-rajan-3209792)

[101] Umair Muhammad, Confronting Injustice: Social Activism in the Age of Individualism - Haymarket Books (https://www.google.co.in/books/edition/Confronting_Injustice/s1WvDQAAQBAJ?hl=en&gbpv=1)

production lines to produce loads of goods, just as there is pressure on the middle class to consume those goods. Overexposure to popular culture and advertisements has meant that the middle class has fully internalized the core message of consumerism: that one's social status is equal to the goods one buys.

This false sense of identity creates a *false consciousness*[102] that is *"counterintuitive to their economic, social, and political self-interests,"*[103] according to Marx. False consciousness is a tricky thing to deal with. It not only distracts people from the socio-political and economic reality at play, but also creates competition among members of the same group for better social and political status.

What they fail to realize is that their experiences, struggles, and interests are common. However, instead of forming a united front, they remain alienated and disarrayed.

One could argue that the fusion of individualism and consumerism has not only undermined individuality but also dealt a fatal blow to social activism. Moreover, with *social media echo chambers*[104] firmly in place, it has become

---

[102] False Consciousness - University of Michigan (http://www-personal.umd.umich.edu/~delittle/iess%20false%20consciousness%20V2.htm)

[103] Understanding Karl Marx's Class Consciousness and False Consciousness - ThoughtCo (https://www.thoughtco.com/class-consciousness-3026135)

[104] What is an Echo Chamber? - Digital Media Literacy (https://edu.gcfglobal.org/en/digital-media-literacy/what-is-an-

increasingly difficult to debunk the distorted view of reality that people have embraced.

Social media algorithms, designed to maximize user engagement, prioritize content that aligns with users' existing political beliefs. Although this benefits social media companies, it further reinforces people's delusions, resulting in apathy and inaction.

***

This situation is reminiscent of Orwell's 1984, in which the majority of the population is composed of Proles, who constitute roughly 85% of the population.

According to Orwell, the Proles are engaged in *"Heavy physical work, the care of home and children, petty quarrels with neighbours, films, football, beer and, above all, gambling filled up the horizon of their minds."*[105]

This sounds familiar even today, many decades after Orwell published the novel in 1949.

---

echo-chamber/1/#)
[105] George Orwell, Nineteen Eighty-Four

8

THE INTERPLAY BETWEEN VOCABULARY AND THOUGHT: AN OVERVIEW

"1984" portrays numerous instances where language is utilized to distort meaning and restrict thought. But, is there really a correlation between one's vocabulary and the extent to which one can think? In simpler terms, does having an extensive vocabulary lead to having profound thoughts or insights? Or, is language essential for comprehending reality or being politically conscious?

One school of thought, represented by linguist Lee Whorf, believes that people can have different perspectives on the world due to "differences in their language."[106] If language is distorted, then it

---

[106] Does The Language I Speak Influence The Way I Think? - Linguistic Society of America (https://www.linguisticsociety.org/content/does-language-i-speak-influence-way-i-think)

can distort a speaker's worldview, as it is no longer the same original language.

However, it is not just language that shapes how people think; culture also plays a role. This includes lifestyle, colors, symbols, and even the people we associate with, all of which can influence how we perceive reality.

Linguistic relativity suggests that *"the structure of a language influences its speakers' worldview or cognition, and thus people's perceptions are relative to their spoken language."*[107]

This concept helps to explain the political implications of doublespeak in 1984. When a specific political group imposes vocabulary that leans a certain way on people, it can have serious consequences, as it restricts their worldview.

Language used in response to external events can reveal one's political leanings. Research conducted at Stanford University "analyzed 4.4 million tweets in response to 21 different mass shootings" and found that:

"Republicans were also 25 percent more likely than Democrats to write "terrorist" in tweets about the shootings in which the shooter was African American, Hispanic or Middle Eastern. Democrats

---

[107] Wikipedia contributors. (2023, April 29). Linguistic relativity. In Wikipedia, The Free Encyclopedia. Retrieved 13:21, May 4, 2023, from
https://en.wikipedia.org/w/index.php?title=Linguistic_relativity&oldid=1152281009

were 25 percent more likely to use the same word when they tweeted about shootings in which the shooter was white."[108]

Language can have a profound impact on how we interpret and respond to situations,[109] and this is closely linked to our internalization of language and its political leanings. When a particular language is consistently reinforced, it can shape our habits of thought and action[110] to a significant degree.

***

In the realm of politics, the language employed by politicians can shape public opinion. During Trump's presidency, language often embodied deception and was tailored to different groups of people. To his devotees, he made one set of statements that were blatant lies, only to later disown them when pressed for evidence. This flexibility was made possible by the use of

---

[108] New Stanford Research Shows Difference In Language Used By Republicans And Democrats - Stanford News (https://news.stanford.edu/2019/06/25/analyzing-tweets-republicans-democrats/)

[109] Relationship Between Thinking & Language. (2017, September 4). Retrieved from https://study.com/academy/lesson/relationship-between-thinking-language.html.

[110] Language and Thinking - Lumen (https://courses.lumenlearning.com/waymaker-psychology/chapter/reading-language-and-thought/)

doublespeak, which allowed him to misrepresent the truth in order to "gain unwavering support and control over" his ardent followers.[111]

This blatant disregard for truth is the first step in the direction of totalitarianism. Trump's flowery language, combined with simplistic promises to restore America's past glory, resonated with millions of Americans, leading them to vote for him.

However, Lane Greene makes an important distinction, as he argues that George Orwell got one thing wrong about language and politics: *the belief that simple language would make it impossible for politicians to hide the truth.*

This approach does not seem to have worked out in practice, particularly in the cases of Trump and Brexit. Both instances utilized plain language to sway voters in their favor, and the truth was obscured rather than revealed when language was stripped of deception.

"Brexit's proponents toured the country in a bus that featured the slogan "We send the EU £350m a week. Let's fund the NHS [UK National Health Service] instead. Vote Leave."

"The £350m figure was fake; it was a net number that didn't take into account the money

---

[111] Ivy McKay, Donald Trump and Doublespeak: An Unsettling Precursor to the Dystopian Society of George Orwell's 1984, University of Central Florida (https://stars.library.ucf.edu/cgi/viewcontent.cgi?article=1091&context=urj)

Britain got back from the EU … But when supporters of staying in the EU pointed this out, they were dismissed as "elites" with no standing to talk about what the real British people—sick of elites—wanted."[112]

Despite lacking elevated language, plain language was effective in swaying public opinion in favor of Trump and Brexit. This shows that language doesn't necessarily have to be complex to manipulate facts, and that the disregard for truth can make any language effective in achieving its aims.

"Orwell fails to consider that public figures can use concise language to communicate insincere ideas more persuasively. People can easily understand an uncomplicated sentence without the need to think about it deeply. Simple language, like Trump's, inspires automatic thought. Trump's ability to use concise language to lie more convincingly represents a possibility Orwell never considered."[113]

Those who were accustomed to the ornate language of politics might have been surprised by the plain and straightforward rhetoric employed by Trump and pro-Brexit leaders. This could have

---

[112] Lane Greene, Orwell Thought That Plain Political Language Could Save Us. Then Came Trump. - Politico Magazine (https://www.politico.com/magazine/story/2018/11/10/donald-trump-george-orwell-222404/)

[113] Melissa Bo-Ya Feng, Orwell, Trump, and Twitter: Reexamining the Relationship Between Politics and Language (https://wp.nyu.edu/mercerstreet/2021-2022/orwell-trump-and-twitter-reexamining-the-relationship-between-politics-and-language/)

played a role in their susceptibility to manipulation. The language used may have sounded truthful, but in reality, it was deceiving people who were not concerned with the facts.

9

LINGUISTIC MANIPULATION AND POLITICAL CONDITIONING IN 1984 AND BEYOND

When autocratic rulers use barbaric means to silence dissenting voices, people tend to overlook the role of language as a hegemonic tool. The spectacle of someone being gunned down in a public square can be a smokescreen that distracts from a more insidious attack on people's psyches. The violence and gore of such an event can divert attention from the more significant and sophisticated assault that is happening at the level of language and discourse.

In our current era, anyone with an Internet connection and a smartphone can express their opinion. However, the words and manner in which they do so are often politically influenced. Depending on the type of response certain words elicit, individuals may be inclined to use language that aligns with the dominant ideology, in order to garner approval from the state.

Self-censorship often leads to a homogeneity of expressed opinions, which is difficult to achieve in a democratic society. This monotony is indicative of living under a regime rather than a government, as a regime is focused on consolidating power while a government prioritizes the well-being of its people. In a regime, the uniformity of voiced opinions is a clear sign of the government's centralization of power.

If a political entity feels that its power is being threatened, it may turn to democratic means such as holding elections, *but there is a catch*. It may support the notion of ballet supremacy while simultaneously limiting the space for rational discussion and political opposition. By doing so, the entity disenfranchises voters and takes away their freedom to choose representatives who can represent their interests.

A significant amount of money is spent to sway the opinions of media personnel, journalists, and high-profile bureaucrats through lucrative salaries and special privileges, such as access to corridors of power.

As a result, they often parrot the official line verbatim, without any critical analysis or independent thought. This repetition can quickly become habitual, and when the same message is broadcast 24/7, its impact can be alarming to imagine.

When loudmouthed news anchors sing the

praises of their masters, no blood is shed. However, it is not out of the question that such actions could provoke violent reactions that result in bloodshed.

The state uses various channels, such as social media, traditional media, and newspapers, to propagate its language and ideas. So, it is essential to consider the role of language as a hegemonic tool, as it is often overlooked.

Orwell's observation that man is *"essentially linguistic"*[114] is particularly relevant today. Language not only shapes our perceptions but also influences how we interpret and understand the world around us.

This becomes especially problematic in a generation where people are glued to their mobile phone screens, lacking the time or space for contemplation. In such a scenario, the dangers of being overly influenced by language become all the more pronounced.

Even autocratic leaders understand that it is impossible to eliminate language or replace it. Instead, they use manipulation as a tool to restrict the "free play"[115] of language and ideas. The

---

[114] Language and Ideology in Orwell's 1984
Steven Blakemore
Social Theory and Practice, Vol. 10, No. 3, A Special Issue:
Orwell's 1984 (Fall 1984), pp. 349-356 (8 pages)
https://www.jstor.org/stable/23556571
[115] Freeplay, Oxford Reference
(https://www.oxfordreference.com/display/10.1093/oi/authorit
y.20110803095834423;jsessionid=AA48A99DEF7270FF5345725

dichotomy of "you are either with us or against us" is often used to limit critical thinking and analysis. Logical reasoning, which involves weighing different arguments before drawing conclusions, is discouraged. In this way, leaders seek to control the options available to people and limit their capacity for independent thought, thereby action.

The war in Iraq was supported by many people based on a media narrative about the presence of "weapons of mass destruction" that were never found. There was no room for discussion or questioning, and the government was able to get away with its lies to the American and world citizens.

The transition from 'Oldspeak' to 'Newspeak' is a gradual but dangerous process. It often starts with the introduction of 'alternative facts' that may not be true but are eventually accepted as historical truth. As a result, evidence that contradicts these 'alternative facts' may be erased from people;s minds, leading to a distorted understanding of reality.

Two contrasting realities, one real and the other fake, are often presented to the public, and people are asked to choose between them. For many, this may seem like a hallmark of democracy, as two opposing viewpoints are given equal media coverage.

However, what they fail to realize is that this is

32D15C929)

often a trap, designed to lure them into accepting a false narrative. Over time, this false narrative may gain momentum, and eventually become the dominant narrative, reinforced by round-the-clock media coverage. Once this happens, it can be difficult to turn back, and people may find themselves trapped in a world of lies and deception.

Introducing a new language is similar to the introduction of a new currency in the aftermath of demonetization. You may have bundles of old notes, but they become worthless after new currency replaces them. It is a forceful systemic change that is hard to get past. In 1984, it is not the money that is replaced. The Party introduces a new language in the form of 'Newspeak' to replace 'Oldspeak'.

Replacing old currency with new has economic repercussions, but as long as you can buy your basic necessities with the new currency, you are not losing its value by replacing it.

However, language is not just a medium of exchange like currency. It shapes our thoughts, perceptions, and beliefs. So, the introduction of a new language like Newspeak is not just a change in medium but a change in the way we think and communicate.

Language plays a unique role in our lives, as it is not just a tool for communication but also a vital aspect of our cultural identity. When a language is replaced, it is not just a matter of learning new words and phrases, but also losing a part of our cultural heritage. The replacement of language can have sinister undertones, especially when it is done to meet political ends.

Language is the medium through which we connect with our history, customs, and beliefs. It is a shared wisdom that makes us part of a larger reality. When language is taken away or distorted, we lose our mental acuity, sanity, and sensibility. We become disconnected from our own feelings, reality, and history, creating a sense of emptiness and vacuum.

Orwell's 1984 illustrates this point through the introduction of Newspeak, a new language designed to incorporate the party ideology into the vocabulary of its speakers. In this way, the party could erase the old language and write its new propagandistic language on people's mind, which is now a clean slate. The words in Newspeak are selected in a way that reinforces the party's ideology, and thus, restricts the range of ideas that can be expressed.

In short, the replacement of language is a serious matter that goes beyond mere semantics. It has the potential to erase cultural identities, restrict the range of ideas, and undermine our connection to reality and history.

When the historical roots are erased, it becomes challenging to make informed decisions in the present. You may have to continually learn and relearn to arrive at a system of thought that doesn't overwhelm you and helps you make informed choices. However, the problem is that you are constantly distracted by various forms of diversions, leaving little time for deep contemplation or critical thinking. Without a sense of the past, it is impossible to evaluate whether our nation's trajectory is positive or negative because there is no historical reference point left to compare it with.

Eliminating all traces of Hitler from people's consciousness would render them incapable of recognizing and opposing fascism. Without a historical framework and firsthand experience, people would struggle to identify the early signs of fascism, which often involve the distortion of historical reality through the constant propagation of propaganda.

When historical records are destroyed or distorted, history loses its authenticity and becomes merely a linguistic construction, regardless of whether or not it corresponds to actual evidence or records. The Party takes advantage of this gap by inventing lies and extrapolations to fill the void.

At first, Winston had a fragmented sense of his historical roots, but once they were eliminated and replaced with Newspeak, the language invented by the Party, Winston began to conform to the Party's ideology. When this is done on a mass scale, the Party can act with impunity, using brute force without fear of public reaction, resentment, or resistance, as the Party is confident that the masses will support its actions.

All of this is accomplished through the manipulation of language. As people are inundated with lies and propaganda, they are unable to discern the truth and fail to react to their own oppression. The state in Orwell's 1984 uses language to *"tear human minds to pieces and put them back together in the new shape of your own choosing."*[116] The ultimate goal is to use *"party language [to] confine human thought"*[117] to the point where war is peace and freedom is slavery.

The constant refinement of language in Newspeak eventually leads speakers to lose their sense of the past. Each time a new edition of Newspeak is introduced, the previous version becomes obsolete, and with it, the words and meanings that were associated with it. Consequently, the only worldview that remains is the one provided by the Party, which is based entirely on its own semantic vocabulary.

***

Instead of getting caught up in the dichotomy

---

[116] George Orwell, Nineteen Eighty-Four
[117] Language and Ideology in Orwell's 1984
Steven Blakemore
Social Theory and Practice, Vol. 10, No. 3, A Special Issue:
Orwell's 1984 (Fall 1984), pp. 349-356 (8 pages)
https://www.jstor.org/stable/23556571

of "my truth" versus "your truth" or "my history" versus "your history", it is crucial to transcend this dichotomy and recognize the objective truth.

Rejecting all history as a lie propagated by biased historians is also a dangerous perspective, as Orwell pointed out, as it can play into the hands of the ruling regime. Such a blanket rejection would not only disregard pseudo-history but also neutral and fact-based history, ultimately leading to the surrender of intellectual abilities.

"Winston Smith is a prototype of man deliberately being remade by political and technological forces."[118]

Ingsoc party members are encouraged to inhibit their private thoughts and feelings, which requires taming both biological and psychological impulses. Anything that might provide an individual with a sense of personal identity is under attack, as the party seeks to produce mass conformity.

As previously discussed, the vocabulary of Newspeak is used to politically condition individuals and prevent deviance from state policy. "Totalitarian power has a real stake in language and aims to dominate it."[119]

In Orwell's 1984, exhibiting unease, doubt, or any other form of conscious or unconscious

---

[118] Feder, L. (1983). Selfhood, Language, and Reality: George Orwell's "Nineteen Eighty-Four." The Georgia Review, 37(2), 392–409. http://www.jstor.org/stable/41398529

[119] Courtine, J.-J., & Willett, L. (1986). A Brave New Language: Orwell's Invention of "Newspeak" in 1984. SubStance, 15(2), 69–74. https://doi.org/10.2307/3684756

reaction can lead to trouble. Therefore, individuals must carefully apportion their biological and psychological responses to avoid betraying any signs of dissent. This alienates people from one another and breaks all ties of kinship, as individuals cannot risk exposing one another to the regime.

Language has the power to conceal any inner rebellious thoughts brewing up inside one's mind. Deceptive language can hide ulterior motives from even the most astute observers. Hence, for a totalitarian regime, it is imperative to control language, so that people can only think thoughts generated by the party-approved vocabulary.

In Orwell's words, this process "fills you with ourselves,"[120] as O'Brien put it to Winston, effectively meaning that individuals begin to think in the language of Big Brother, as Winston Smith did later on.

Under normal circumstances, language in its pristine form enables individuals to think freely without restrictions. However, totalitarian regimes consider free thought as an act of rebellion.

What an individual thinks determines the language they use, and the language they have internalized influences the thoughts they can think. In 1984, Big Brother prefers the latter proposition, where thought processing is restrained rather than left unbridled.

Newspeak, therefore, is the expression of

---

[120] George Orwell, Nineteen Eighty-Four

"linguistic determinism," which makes political conditioning easier until people start obeying the authorities unquestioningly and *"accept all propaganda as reality."*[121]

Although it is typical to enrich vocabulary to broaden the intellectual horizons of speakers, the 1984 regime opposes it. With fewer words available, speakers face the dilemma of how to express their thoughts without the corresponding vocabulary. This predicament gave rise to the "orthodoxy of thought" where people are constrained to think in the language of the party ideology, and any divergence is labeled "thoughtcrime."

Furthermore, the narrowed vocabulary leads to "fragile memory" with no words to record or articulate past and present experiences. The 1984 language project covertly incorporates Newspeak into everyday language through media and broadcasts, avoiding direct imposition.

Although not mandatory, it acquires an unofficial official status and exerts influence on public diction, facilitating the widespread adoption of Newspeak.

Social media has emerged as a platform where truth is often discredited, and dissidents are mercilessly trolled to bury voices of reason. Journalists can be sued on false charges of

---

[121] Jem Berkes, Language as the "Ultimate Weapon" in Nineteen Eighty-Four
(https://berkes.ca/archive/berkes_1984_language.html)

spreading fake news, but social media trolls often face no consequences for their actions.[122]

[122] John Berthelsen, The meaning of words: Orwell, Didion, Trump and the Death of Language - Salon (https://www.salon.com/2021/12/27/the-meaning-of-words-orwell-joan-didion-and-the-of-language/)

10
FROM FICTION TO REALITY: REVISITING 1984 IN THE AGE OF TRUMP

The storming of the *Capitol in Washington*[123] was a watershed moment in American history. It marked a turning point where the U.S., which had claimed to be lighting the candle of democracy in Middle Eastern and Latin American countries[124] was now facing the threat of having that same candle snuffed out within its own borders.

The events of the Capitol insurrection revealed

---

[123] Duignan, B. (2023, May 5). January 6 U.S. Capitol attack. Encyclopedia Britannica.
https://www.britannica.com/event/January-6-U-S-Capitol-attack

[124] Steven Gilber, The U.S. Policy of Democracy Promotion in Latin America - Eastern Michigan University
(https://commons.emich.edu/cgi/viewcontent.cgi?article=1147&context=honors)

the vulnerability of U.S. democracy,[125] despite the country's claims of strength and stability.

Nearly 29 million people tuned in to watch news coverage of that fateful day,[126] and the message was clear: when leaders neglect their constitutional duty, chaos ensues. Trump's refusal to concede defeat was a reflection of his delusional mindset, and his supporters fell prey to his false claims of a stolen mandate.

Inciting a mob without resorting to 'alternative facts' is an impossible feat. Trump understood the hypnotic power of language and used it to cultivate a cult following. Just like Newspeak, the language used in George Orwell's novel 1984, Trump's rhetoric can prompt impulsive actions without much critical thinking. The Capitol insurrection was a manifestation of this dangerous phenomenon.

Orwell's 1984 remains prescient not only in the American context but also provides a valuable contextual foundation for understanding how totalitarian and dystopian societies[127] operate, and

---

[125] Wilson Lievano and Josh Coe, The Capitol Riots Showed U.S. Democracy's Vulnerability. How Does That Affect Its Global Influence? - The GroundTruth Project (https://thegroundtruthproject.org/capitol-breach-demonstrated-u-s-democracys-vulnerability-how-does-that-affect-americas-global-influence-president-trump-impeachment/)

[126] Rick Porter, Capitol Insurrection Drives Huge Audience to TV News - The Hollywood Reporter (https://www.hollywoodreporter.com/tv/tv-news/capitol-insurrection-drives-huge-audience-to-tv-news-4113264/)

[127] Andrew Liptak, Orwell Would Be Horrified by the Right Wing's Use of Orwellian - Slate

how language and technology are employed to suppress free, independent, and rational thinking.

When truth is obscured by layers of deception, and the path to discovering the truth is difficult, time-consuming, and hindered by state oppression, people may prefer to accept the veiled version of events. This alternate reality gains traction, and individuals become mentally enslaved and engage in self-surveillance in addition to state surveillance, as discussed in previous chapters.

The space for journalists to operate is increasingly restricted, and those who have the courage to penetrate through the veils of deception to uncover the truth are often physically eliminated. In 2022 alone, 67 journalists were killed, and 41 of them were murdered "in direct connection with their work."[128] "The rate of impunity for journalist killings" according to UNESCO, "remains shockingly high at 86%."[129]

The motive behind killing journalists is twofold: first, to serve as a warning to those who seek to uncover the truth, and second, to ensure that the

---

(https://slate.com/technology/2021/01/orwellian-1984-donald-trump-jr-josh-hawley.html)

[128] Deadly year for journalists as killings rose sharply in 2022 - Committee to Protect Journalists (https://cpj.org/reports/2023/01/deadly-year-for-journalists-as-killings-rose-sharply-in-2022/)

[129] UNESCO: Killings of Journalists up 50% in 2022, Half Targeted Off Duty (https://www.unesco.org/en/articles/unesco-killings-journalists-50-2022-half-targeted-duty)

truth remains hidden. Who would risk their life to challenge the government when dissent is met with violence?

While some brave individuals have sought to uncover the truth and paid the ultimate price at the hands of fascist regimes, many have chosen strategic silence to avoid the wrath of the ruling party. Some have even collaborated with the government to reap benefits and promote their agenda. Authoritarian regimes recognize that "government-controlled media is an effective tool to shape public opinion,"[130] and they use it accordingly.

Despite initial hopes that social media would democratize media and promote free speech, it has instead become a tool for the state to crack down on dissenting voices and amplify pro-government propaganda. This has resulted in an erosion of free speech rather than an enhancement of it.

The technology behind social media has been co-opted by the state to further their political agenda and spew hatred against political opponents, minority groups, and "people critical of their sectarian idea."[131]

In India, Facebook has become a breeding

---

[130] Pan, J., Shao, Z., & Xu, Y. (2022). How government-controlled media shifts policy attitudes through framing. Political Science Research and Methods, 10(2), 317–332. http://doi.org/10.1017/psrm.2021.35

[131] Siddhartha Deb, The killing of Gauri Lankesh - Columbia Journalism Review (https://www.cjr.org/special_report/gauri-lankesh-killing.php)

ground for hate speech against Muslims and other minority groups, fanning the flames of sectarianism and inciting violence.

A diatribe delivered by Yati Narsinghanand, a Hindu priest in India, was captured on video and shared on Facebook, receiving over 32 million views. Within the same month, his speech: *"I will use weapons. I am telling each and every Muslim, Islam will be eradicated from the country one day,"*[132] was posted on Facebook and garnered over 59 million views, yet Facebook did not take it down.

The Facebook whistleblower, Frances Haugen, shed light on the issue in her complaint filed with the US Securities and Exchange Commission. She cited an internal document of the company titled, "Adversarial Harmful Networks – India Case Study" to support her claims. The document stated:

"RSS [Indian nationalist organisation Rashtriya Swayamsevak Sangh] Users, Groups, and Pages promote fear-mongering, anti-Muslim narratives targeted pro-Hindu populations with V&I [violence and inciting] intent."[133]

The subservience of social media companies to authoritarian regimes sets a dangerous precedent.

---

[132] Facebook In India: Why Is It Still Allowing Hate Speech Against Muslims? - Middle East Eye (https://www.middleeasteye.net/big-story/facebook-meta-india-muslims-allow-hate-speech)

[133] 'Facebook Knew Rss Promotes Anti-Muslim Narratives But Took Little Action', Whistleblower Says - The Print (https://theprint.in/tech/facebook-knew-rss-promotes-anti-muslim-narratives-but-took-little-action-whistleblower-says/747033/)

They either cower before the powers that be or prioritize profit over impartial content moderation. Perhaps it's a combination of both. Hateful posts can be lucrative for these companies, generating extraordinary traction, high levels of user engagement, and substantial profits.

On the other hand, the rules against hate speech of these companies *"tend to favor elites and governments over grassroots activists and racial* [and religious] *minorities. In so doing, they serve the business interests of the global company, which relies on national governments not to block its service to their citizens."*[134]

This creates a sort of partnership where the state's proxies are given a free hand to spread hate while *"posts by activists and journalists in disputed territories such as Palestine, Kashmir, Crimea and Western Sahara"* are deleted. Furthermore, user data is often shared with the government in exchange for a favored entry into other sectors of the operating market.

Trump's use of Twitter has been compared to Ingsoc's use of Telescreens in 1984. His tweets fomented polarization, spewed hate, sowed distrust, and spread disinformation until January 8, 2021, when he was handed a lifetime ban from the platform. With just a tweet labeling information he

---

[134] Facebook's Secret Censorship Rules Protect White Men From Hate Speech But Not Black Children - ProPublica (https://www.propublica.org/article/facebook-hate-speech-censorship-internal-documents-algorithms)

didn't like as "fake news," Trump undermined its credibility, a tactic that was often picked up by his 88 million followers who also deemed it fake news.

According to Sam Woolley, the director of propaganda research at the University of Texas, *"Trump's primary use of Twitter has been to spread propaganda and manipulate public opinion. He used Twitter to delegitimize information or to delegitimize the positions of his opponents."*[135]

Of note are the 36 posts he made about election fraud, which collectively received 22.6 million likes and 3.9 million retweets. These posts played a role in inciting the violent insurrection by Trump supporters at the Capitol on January 6, 2021.

The prevalence of hateful expression on social media, particularly directed towards *"people of African descent … advocacy of national, racial and religious hatred that constitutes incitement to discrimination and violence, as well as racism on social media"*[136] is a stark reminder of the toxic environment that has developed within human societies.

The advocacy of national, racial, and religious hatred is not only discriminatory but also constitutes incitement to violence, and its widespread presence on social media is a testament

---

[135] Trump's Election Lies Were Among his Most Popular Tweets - CNBC (https://www.cnbc.com/2021/01/13/trump-tweets-legacy-of-lies-misinformation-distrust.html)

[136] 'Urgent Need' for More Accountability from Social Media Giants to Curb Hate Speech: UN Experts (https://news.un.org/en/story/2023/01/1132232)

to the state of human rights under fascist regimes across the world. This is reminiscent of the dystopian society of Oceania in Orwell's 1984 and demands serious consideration.

Through the above discussion, it is evident that a specific message is favored on social media, even when the divisiveness of its content is apparent. However, to bring about unquestioning submission to a particular patry's view, or to the textual reality it manufactures, the guards drop, and the message slips through.

Millions of social media users pick it up and are shooed away from the objective reality, only to be incarcerated forever in a *Trumpian echo chamber* after consuming what appears to be 280 characters of text.

When lines between fact and fiction are blurred, the malignant influence drives people to discredit experts. Dr. Anthony Fauci, for instance, becomes Dr. Doom Fauci, he has to be protected by US Marshals to evade any attempt on his life following death threats.[137]

"What Trump's gonna do is just declare victory. Right? He's gonna declare victory. But that doesn't mean he's a winner. He's just gonna say he's a winner."[138]

Steve Banon had this conversation three days

---

[137] Trump's Orwellian Plague - The Bulwark
(https://www.thebulwark.com/trumps-orwellian-plague/)
[138] 'Game over': Steve Bannon Audio Reveals Trump Planned to Claim Early Victory - The Guardian
(https://www.theguardian.com/us-news/2022/jul/14/steve-bannon-audio-trump-declare-victory)

before the 2020 U.S. presidential election, and it was leaked to the public. This strategy of using lies to cling to power is reminiscent of Orwell's 1984. When the truth is kept from people and objective facts are erased from their memories, they become vulnerable to manipulation and can fall into any trap with patriotic zeal.

At fault, in the words of Naseem Rakha, "*are those in leadership who lack the spine to say "Trump is dead wrong." Sycophants such as Sens. Mitch McConnell, Lindsey Graham and Ted Cruz, people joined at the hip to Trump and his lies because of their own selfish desires for power and their fear of retribution by the very voters they and Trump have cultivated.*"[139]

***

Unraveling the Interplay Between the Economy, Truth, Ignorance, and Governance in Orwell's 1984

In the beginning of George Orwell's novel 1984, electricity is cut off during the daytime as part of an "economy drive" in preparation for Hate Week.

What is Hate Week? In George Orwell's 1984, it is an indoctrination event where citizens are subjected to simulated violence to stoke their

---

[139] Jan. 6 Committee Reveals Trump's Orwellian Attempt to Win the Election - AZ Mirro
(https://www.azmirror.com/2022/07/27/jan-6-committee-reveals-trumps-orwellian-attempt-to-win-the-election/)

patriotic and nationalistic fervor and channel the resulting anger towards an enemy, real or imagined, created by the State. This is similar to some modern-day newsrooms, where sensationalized coverage can fuel divisive emotions and promote an us-versus-them mentality.

The masses are left in the dark about who their supposed enemy is. The simulated violence broadcasted on telescreens triggers fears of complete annihilation at the hands of an unknown adversary. In a state of emotional frenzy, people blindly rally behind the state-sponsored narrative, effectively consenting to their own subjugation under the guise of legality.

Governments, in the pursuit of defeating the enemy, often introduce socio-political and economic policies that are fundamentally flawed and irrational. However, the masses often bear the burden of these so-called reforms with a misplaced sense of patriotic fervor.

They view the inconvenience caused by these policies as a sacrifice and take pride in enduring them. This delusion allows the ruling powers to manipulate the masses and steer the nation in the direction they desire.

The delusion of the masses enables the ruling dispensation, such as a political party, to intertwine with the State to the extent that the State becomes the Party, and the Party becomes the State. As a result, those in power prioritize preserving the party ideology over serving the public. In some countries, such as India, public funds have been spent on constructing statues that serve no practical purpose, except to promote a particular ideology and its ideologues.

The concept of Hate Week, as depicted in Orwell's novel, was echoed in America during the presidency of Donald J. Trump. His controversial demand for a wall along the Mexican border, which came with a staggering price tag, was touted by him as a necessary measure for the survival of the nation. However, in reality, it served to promote the agenda of far-right and white supremacist ideologies that he espoused, rather than the well-being of the country as a whole.

Governments pursuing economically disastrous policies often face public outrage. In response, they resort to stifling legitimate criticism. Anyone who questions the validity of the policy is subjected to unspeakable acts of physical and psychological violence. In the novel, the ubiquitous presence of Big Brother's picture with the caption "Big Brother Is Watching You" instills fear and terror in the hearts and minds of the people.

In the novel, people believe that everything they do, feel, and think is being scrutinized and monitored by Big Brother. Under this fear, people's opinions are molded, both consciously and unconsciously, in favor of the state-sponsored repression considered essential for national security. Falsehoods are taken as truth, and the real truth is detested, while the most deluded are rewarded with prestigious state honors, adding to the state's farcical crowning glory.

In Orwell's novel, the 'Ministry of Truth' plays a key role in propagating falsehood and lies created by the ruling elite. The ministry's primary responsibility is to find ways to nullify the truth. Its propaganda machinery continuously produces fabricated stories to shape and reshape the public narrative as required, ensuring that public consent remains with them.

In today's world, the role of the 'Ministry of Truth' is taken over by the 'Mass Media', which propagates biases, misinformation, and the ruling dispensation's party lines. Its aim is to keep the people deluded by constantly churning out fabricated stories, shaping and reshaping public opinion as and when needed. The past is also being constantly rewritten, maimed and turned into party propaganda to provide context to something that is illegitimate, something that doesn't even exist.

The state's control over the media and technology enables the easy dissemination of irrational facts and divisive policies. Access to the "true past" is often denied or unnecessarily complicated, and adherence to state-sponsored rhetoric without questioning its credibility is rewarded with a false sense of security and freedom.

In reality, willingly adhering to the state-sponsored rhetoric without questioning its credibility is a form of mental slavery that imposes restrictions on one's thoughts, leading to ignorance. Under despotism, ignorance has become a savior for people from political oppression, and it has become a new norm. It provides strength and ensures protection from state terrorism.

Manipulation of Language

"Every year fewer and fewer words and the range of consciousness always a little smaller ..." George Orwell recognized the power of language as a tool of political oppression and tyranny.

It is intriguing that despite significant technological advancements in recent decades, the 'construct of language' remains difficult to escape. Language shapes our perception and understanding of the world, and for most people, breaking free from its influence is unattainable. The ruling elite continually creates new vocabulary to further their agenda and maintain their grip on power.

Day by day, the ruling elite continues to invent new words to manipulate the minds of billions. With the deeper penetration of social media and the strange nexus between politics and mass media, new phrases and terms become current almost instantaneously. The power holders no longer fear inquisitive journalists because they don't have to answer them. They can easily tweet their thoughts in a few words and turn off comments, avoiding any form of accountability.

Words like 'intellectual terrorism' and 'anti-national' are being used to create confusion and divide public opinion. Intellectuals, scholars, film directors, and academicians who are seen as critics of supreme leaders are often labeled with these epithets to portray them as antagonists in the eyes of the public. Derogatory remarks are often hurled at people who do not align with party ideology.

Technology, Present, and Past

In the novel, Winston rebels against the state's control over history by keeping a diary in which he writes his private thoughts, feelings, and ideas. The act of seeking the truth about the past is considered a transgression by the ruling regime. Similarly, in the present world, access to unbiased history is limited as it is often the government that controls and shapes the narrative of the past.

The manipulation of history is used to shape the present and criminalize certain communities while glorifying others, leading to a distorted and false understanding of the past.

"And when memory failed and written records were falsified—when that happened, the claim of the Party to have improved the conditions of human life had to be accepted, because there did not exist, and never again could exist, any standard against which it could be tested."

The telescreens in the novel 1984 can be seen as a precursor to today's social media platforms. While social media sites provide people with a seemingly safe space to share daily happenings, they are constantly monitored and subjected to unfair censorship. Moreover, the data generated by these platforms is being misused for economic and political benefits by tech companies, highlighting the need for stricter regulations to protect the privacy of individuals.

The scandal involving Cambridge Analytica and its exploitation of the privacy of millions of Facebook users to serve political agendas is evidence of Orwell's prophetic warning. It is a confirmation that whoever controls technology controls people's consciousness and whoever controls the past controls the present. While the identity of Big Brother in the novel is unclear, we can see him in the post-Trump era on Twitter, spreading lies and propaganda on a daily basis.

Denial of Reality

Trump's stance on various issues has often been compared to the themes present in Orwell's works. For instance, on climate change, he has repeatedly denied its existence while taking measures to protect his properties near the coast.

This shows his willingness to prioritize personal interests over the greater good. Moreover, Trump's policies have often been seen as disruptive, such as withdrawing from the Paris Climate Treaty and the nuclear non-proliferation treaty. This kind of behavior can lead to global instability and chaos, as opposed to promoting peace and cooperation among nations.

A Sneak Preview of Trump's America

Donald J. Trump will *build-the-wall* and with it, cold winters shall roast liberal chickens who root for immigrants' rights, dignity, and access to pursue the American dream. But, immigrants' frolicking unhindered on American (and Indian) streets is abhorred by xenophones who vote to power *religious and racial bigots* to have them banned and banished from the United States (and from India, too).

The Mexican wall in the American context would do what the Himalayas have been doing in the East: forcing the wind to retreat. Constructing a huge wall along the Mexican border, impossible for desperate humans running after life to trespass, would safeguard American fortunes from the preying eyes of immigrants.

Yet, amidst all this inhuman cruelty meted out to most battered human souls, President Trump (and his friends in the East) can stir a crowd to erupt in a high-pitched cackle. The world never runs short of clowns whose muse is the misery (of others)!

First things first, like his allies elsewhere, President Trump too appoints a far-right propagandist Julia Hahn from Breitbart, to teach people *real* journalism whose guiding principle is to replace truth with falsehood and information with misinformation. As a second fiddle to Julia Hahn, she is accompanied by Sebastian Gorka, teaching people ways to embrace the alt-right ideology, with a brief *dissection* as follows:

This one is the most common among right-wingers (and liberals alike unfortunately!): hush and shiver when you hear of Islam; Obama and Osama have a secret nexus; swear by Hitler, he's a godfather. Under President Trump (and his friends in the East!), the news doesn't happen, it's manufactured in the White House.

Thank the American media (and India too!) for manufacturing and propagating *black-and-white* news that can be consumed without the need to invest in a color TV, thereby saving the trouble of perceiving the truth in all its complex shades. Truth is blacked out and factual understanding is replaced by rosy hallucinations made even rosier by loudmouthed anchors.

As crows of divisive ideologies have laid their eggs in the safe havens of *white houses and parliaments* and officially tend to with state protocol till each egg is hatched and metamorphosed into a monster ready to spit fire and fury, meek cows find their grounds increasingly being constricted.

Authoritarian regimes are increasingly gaining traction and expanding, yet their upsurge remains imperceptible to most people. The voices that ring the alarm bell are stifled by a manipulated media that aligns itself with those in positions of authority. Power and propaganda have become intertwined, and Trump's presidency is no different from other autocratic leaders flaunting their polarizing ideologies elsewhere.

11

Embracing Hope and Humanism to Overcome Fascism

Humanity is facing a multi-faceted attack on its dignity, leaving little space for solace, whether it be physical, psychological, or spiritual. Media profiling and fascistic economic, political, and social policies have pushed countless individuals into despair and neglect, making the pursuit of redemption seem like a hopeless endeavor. As long as corporate greed, fascism, and rampant consumerism continue to fuel each other, it is challenging to regain the pure space of contemplation and peaceful detachment from the mundane.

Environmental degradation and mental/spiritual degradation are closely linked, and together they are leading to a catastrophic outcome. The spread of disinformation, which is often designed to further certain political or economic agendas, has pushed people to the brink. This has resulted in a frenzy of communal violence, with the powerful elites often siding with the perpetrators of these heinous crimes.

The oppressed, meanwhile, are left to suffer and struggle to survive. This disparity is most evident in the climate crisis, where those who are least responsible for the crisis are often the ones who suffer the most, while the corporations and politicians who are primarily responsible continue to profit. As long as this corporate-political nexus remains intact, it will be difficult to reverse these trends and restore a sense of balance and justice.

The ruling elite is rampant in their misuse of state power, as they have much at stake. True power is held by the people, but it is these same people who are subjected to barbaric use by the powerful class in whose hands this power is vested, and who seek to maintain the status quo at all costs.

Whether it is the suppression of voices of reason at gunpoint or the usurpation of democratic space, those in power cultivate masses steeped in xenophobia and religious-political fanaticism to do their bidding, all in the hopes of righting perceived historical wrongs. Meanwhile, the true vultures at the top of the food chain enjoy all the spoils, relishing in the indiscriminate consumption of the politically Other and those on the opposite end of the spectrum - allies without benefits.

The act of questioning the state is often met with severe consequences, and those who attempt it may find themselves sacrificed on the altar of power. Even if you manage to ask a few questions without incurring the wrath of the state, you may still be used as a pawn in the political game when it suits those in power. Meanwhile, the gods of the power corridors feast on your flesh, indifferent to your fate. Even if you claim the right to question, the state retains the privilege of remaining silent and maintaining its hold on power.

The world today is witnessing the rise of a new type of hero, one who is characterized by hatred, ultra-nationalism, racism, and staunch neoliberalism. This hero is enabled by disruptive policies pursued by politicians, and their politics is marked by anti-intellectualism, anti-humanism, and anti-environmentalism. Intellectuals are being humiliated, disgraced, and charged with intellectual terrorism, all in order to keep the masses deluded. This delusion creates a sense of euphoria that clouds the intellect.

The current state of affairs has left us with a difficult choice between hope and despair. Literature has the power to lift us out of despair and instill hope, by offering insights into the human condition and teaching us about the resilience of the human spirit. Through literature, we can learn valuable lessons about life and humanity, and be inspired to confront the challenges that confront us.

I am not here to justify the need for reading novels. Doing so would make it seem like an apology rather than a justification for novels as vessels of complex truths, despite being fictional. I have no intention of defending the novel in the following paragraphs, but I will note that ambiguity in human affairs has become increasingly prevalent. As a result, attempting to isolate a particular theme and decipher its underlying ideology may not always be a worthwhile pursuit.

Diving into murky waters may make them murkier, but there is always the chance of catching a fish or two by sheer luck. Denying this possibility would be undemocratic. However, when human affairs are explored in depth and rendered into a cohesive plot through a novel, it can clear the tide and reveal the troubled waters. Novels have a remarkable ability to expand the canvas of chaotic and crisis situations and reveal multiple meanings that were previously obscured.

***

As regards consumerism, will creating more industries and producing more goods help combat consumerism, or will it exacerbate the problem? Is economic growth the solution to poverty, or can we find a way to increase our prosperity without being driven by self-interest?

Eliminating greed may not be feasible, but is there a way to ensure that we don't succumb to it at the expense of others? It's unrealistic to wait for the pie to grow and then deny oneself a slice, especially when those who have contributed to its creation are unaware of our selfish desires. When in positions of power, it's challenging not to succumb to the temptation to claim the entire pie for oneself. It's the monopolization of resources by a privileged few that results in the majority's destitution.

The Victorian liberal doctrine that advocates for the 'free play of individualism always working out for the best' does not seem to hold true in the case of capitalism. Granting an individual the freedom to engage in free trade has enabled only a select few to amass large sums of money while contributing little to the society at large. Its short-term benefits are outweighed by its long-term drawbacks.

An Oxfam report highlights India's income inequality, with 1% of the Indian elites controlling 73% of the country's wealth - almost the entire pie. The accumulation of wealth often leads to unethical interference in policy-making and governance. The monopolization of resources by a few results in overexploitation of natural resources. While the wealthy enjoy their extravagant lifestyles, a significant proportion of the population languishes in poverty, often left homeless and exposed to harsh environments exacerbated by climate change.

Selfishness is detrimental to humanity, particularly when it disregards the limitations of human efforts. When a leader prioritizes personal interests over their presidential duties, it is an act of greed. For example, when former US President Trump denies climate change but pursued the construction of embankments to protect his coastal properties from sea-level rise, it demonstrated a willful act of greed that favored the individual over the people.

Therefore, increasing the size of the pie may be a rational solution, but ensuring the equal distribution of the pie, regardless of its size, is a matter of morality.

The quote by O'Neill, an American playwright, *"If a man wants to be happy in this life, he must reconcile himself to its limitations,"* implies the need to reach a stage in life where one acknowledges that they have had enough for themselves and should redirect their fortune towards the collective good. This means ensuring the welfare of the less fortunate and downtrodden, which depends on the moral stance of the person, rather than just rationality. If rationality is solely focused on the survival of the fittest, it leaves the poor and marginalized sections of society vulnerable to be trampled upon by the elite.

***

Radical individualism has become a new religion for humanity, promoting the idea that life is meant to be 'solitary, poor, nasty, brutish thing.' The pursuit of power and wealth has become its central tenet, fueling an unquenchable desire for more that persists until death. However, this pursuit leads only to disorder and conflict, as everyone strives to amass as much power as possible, leading to a never-ending cycle of competition and strife.

Even more concerning is the idea of

"non-interference" in matters of social distress and industrial conditions, which is a fundamental principle of radical individualism. Its political ramifications are even more perilous. Building walls to keep immigrants away from American shores and in other instances calling them "termites" is unacceptable. Poverty has become a shameful stigma that receives little public support despite causing immense suffering.

"Every man is the prisoner of his private inner world," in which he cocoons himself. However, literature has the power to break down the walls of such cocoons - be they racial, political, social, or religious. Literature can serve as a bridge that spans the gulf between individual consciousnesses, allowing readers to step into someone else's situation and be moved by the emotions of others.

What is remarkable and inspiring is the response to Trump's immigration ban and the Citizenship Amendment Act in India, where people came out in large numbers to defy the ban and welcome immigrants to the US, and support anti-CAA protests in India. Other events, including the Women's March on Washington, Black Lives Matter protests, farmers protesting against farm laws in India, demonstrate that many are aware and not easily distracted enough to accept all government actions at face value. These instances offer hope in the face of fascism's attempt to silence voices advocating for political, cultural, and linguistic diversity.

Humanity's hope lies in the continual battle between the angelic and demonic selves within each individual, without blindly submitting to either. As William Blake states, "Without contraries is no progression," and David Daiches adds, "The true vision cannot come to the innocent, nor can it come to those who accept the distortions of experience; those distortions must be known and transcended."

***

From a humanistic perspective, there exists an essential human nature that is innate, universal, and independent of historical and cultural differences. Across hostile borders, one can find individuals who exhibit exceptional human values that transcend conflict, prejudice, discriminatory policies, and media propaganda. These instances offer hope for a better future and remind us of the power of our shared humanity.

Existential philosophy, popularized by writers like Albert Camus, offers a different perspective on life than humanism. Existentialists view human life as an existence that is 'both anguished and absurd.' They argue that an individual is not an independent entity but rather a product of social construction. According to existential philosophy, a human being is a hopeless case who cannot be improved, chiseled, or decorated to embody humane values, thereby closing all doors to redemption.

However, according to Chomsky, the belief in *"innate and determinate human nature can provide the grounds on which to resist impositions on human liberty."* Chomsky's commitment to humanism and innate human nature offers hope that we can embody humane values, and inspires the fight against despots, for human rights and against human rights abuses.

In the fight against state-sponsored crime, whether activists win or lose may be less consequential than the moral victory they achieve along the way. Breaking down walls that block the richness and diversity of life experiences is crucial for humanity. It is this pursuit that holds the most value, regardless of the outcome of any particular battle.

*****

Even George Orwell's 1984 highlights the crises of humanism, and overcoming this crisis could potentially eliminate the consequences of fascism. Fascism embitters people and alienates them from one another. By keeping people divided, the ruling powers can continue to commit barbaric acts and exploit national and natural resources.

However, if we recognize each other's humanity and fill our hearts with hope and humility, we may be able to develop an action plan that renders fascism irrelevant. Orwell was a champion of humanism, remaining committed to essential "ideals of human dignity, reason, and freedom."[140]

The various forces at play - political, cultural, economic, and technological - have the power to reduce people's lives to mere survival, as depicted in Orwell's 1984. Under such conditions, the search for meaning and salvation through factual truth can seem futile. Instead, people turn to the latest gadgets, high fashion, and expensive brands as a source of liberation. The consequence of this consumerism is a rise in thuggish profiteering and hate-mongering, happening right under our noses.

Embracing humanism can be a powerful antidote to the destructive forces of fascism, individualism, and consumerism that threaten to rob us of our humanity and purpose. By recognizing and valuing each other's inherent worth and dignity, we can build stronger, more compassionate communities that are less susceptible to the appeal of authoritarianism and hate.

Humanism reminds us that life is not about accumulating possessions or achieving status, but about finding meaning and fulfillment through our connections with others and our contributions to the world. As we strive to live by these values, we can create a brighter future for ourselves and generations to come.

---

[140] Dwan, D. (2020). Orwell and Humanism. In N. Waddell (Ed.), The Cambridge Companion to Nineteen Eighty-Four (pp. 64–78). chapter, Cambridge: Cambridge University Press. http://doi.org/10.1017/9781108887090.005

12

Reading is a Political Act: Fostering Critical Thinking and Countering Meta Narrative

Reading books in today's day and age can be a powerful political act because it has the potential to promote critical thinking in readers, leading them to question the dominant narratives of politics and history that the government may want them to accept unquestioningly.

Reading entails examining the messages that political actors are conveying, understanding their motivations, and interpreting their actions in light of the broader political and social currents of the time.

By cultivating the habit of reading, one can swim through the increasing complexity of political messaging and gain a deeper understanding of the issues that are shaping our world today. Whether we are analyzing the actions of a government, a political party, or a social movement, reading books is essential for making informed decisions and engaging in meaningful ways with larger political discourse.

Books have a potential for transmitting ideas and shaping public opinion. Throughout history, books have been banned, censored, and burned by governments seeking to control the flow of information and shape public perception.

When readers engage with books, they are exposed to a wide range of ideas and perspectives, many of which may be different from the dominant narratives put forth by the government or other powerful institutions. By critically examining these different perspectives, readers can develop a more nuanced understanding of the state of politics and history, one that may challenge the official version of events.

Moreover, reading books can promote critical thinking skills, allowing readers to engage with complex issues and develop their own informed opinions. This ability to think critically is essential in a democratic society where citizens are expected to participate in the political process, make informed decisions, and hold those in power accountable.

In addition to promoting critical thinking, reading books can also foster empathy and understanding. By reading books that present diverse perspectives and experiences, readers can develop a deeper appreciation for the challenges faced by those who may be different from themselves. This empathy can lead to greater tolerance and inclusivity, which are essential values for a democratic society.

Arundhati Roy, an Indian author and political activist, has spoken extensively about the power of fiction to convey truth in a way that is often more accessible and resonant than traditional forms of political discourse. In her view, fiction provides a space for alternative perspectives and marginalized voices to be heard, even when the government seeks to control the narrative through censorship or the promotion of party ideology.

In many countries, government interference in school systems has led to the production of new versions of textbooks that are designed to promote a particular political agenda or ideology. This has led to concerns about the accuracy and completeness of the information presented to students, as well as the impact of such ideological indoctrination on young minds.

However, fiction offers a space for the truth to be told in a way that is not subject to government censorship or interference. In her book "The God of Small Things," for example, Roy uses the story of a family in India to explore themes of caste, gender, and colonialism, revealing the complex interplay between personal and political histories that shape our world.

Roy argues that fiction can be a powerful tool

for challenging dominant narratives and providing a voice to those who are often silenced or marginalized. By presenting alternative perspectives and exploring the complexities of human experience, fiction can help to foster empathy and understanding, while also exposing meta narratives.[141]

Readers by *recognizing meta narrative* can discard it, before it is turned into a tool of propaganda that reinforces certain ideologies while marginalizing alternative narratives. As is often the case, meta-narratives serve those in power to maintain their authority, even when their actions are harmful or unjust. Reading books challenges these narratives, as individuals can begin to critically examine the information and come up with their own opinions based on a varied set of perspectives.

Fiction allows for a more personal exploration of complex issues and experiences. By portraying characters and their stories in a way that is grounded in emotional, psychological, and historical truth, fiction can offer readers a deeper understanding of the human impact of dominant narratives.

By allowing readers to see the world through the eyes of characters who are different from

---

[141] Meta narratives refer to the dominant or prevailing cultural or political storylines that shape how we understand the world around us. These narratives are often perpetuated by those in power, and can serve to legitimize certain beliefs or ideologies while marginalizing alternative perspectives.

themselves, fiction can promote a more empathetic and compassionate view of others, thereby challenging *media* stereotypes by giving voice to marginalized groups and highlighting their experiences and perspectives.

Arundhati Roy's novel "The Ministry of Utmost Happiness" challenges the dominant meta-narrative of inclusive India by shedding light on the experiences of marginalized groups excluded from mainstream discourse. Through her novel, Roy highlights the complexity of socio-political landscape in today's india.

By highlighting the persecution of Kashmiris, discrimination against Dalits and hatred for transgenders, Roy interweaves multiple strands into a complex narrative, challenging the monolithic state-sponsored meta narrative. It is her attempt to promote a more just and equitable picture of India's complex reality through her novel.

Similarly, take the example of "Things Fall Apart" by Chinua Achebe that challenges the *colonialist narrative of Africa as a primitive and uncivilized continent* by portraying the complexity and richness of pre-colonial Igbo culture in Nigeria. Or, "The Bluest Eye" by Toni Morrison that rips apart the dominant narrative of white beauty standards through portrayal of the catastrophic effects of internalized racism on the psyche of a young Black girl. Or, for that matter, take the example of "1984" by George Orwell, exploring the dominant political ideology of totalitarianism and the use of propaganda to control the masses.

In short, reading books can broaden our perspectives and diversify our opinions, allowing us to better understand marginalized stories and become more aware of everyday events that may not be covered in the media. Moreover, reading can help us overcome confirmation biases and break free from the echo chambers of social media.

***

Confirmation bias occurs when we seek out information that confirms our existing beliefs, while ignoring information that contradicts them, thereby affecting the way we receive and interpret information. This bias can limit our ability to see the world objectively and prevent us from considering alternative perspectives.

One way to break away from confirmation biases and broaden our worldview is through reading novels. Novels expose us to diverse experiences that can challenge our preoccupations, assumptions, or prejudices, and help us empathize with others and develop a deeper understanding of the complexities of the human experience.

Take, for example, "To Kill a Mockingbird" by Harper Lee. Set in the 1930s in the Southern United States, the novel explores the themes of *racism, prejudice, and injustice*. Through the eyes of the young protagonist, Scout Finch, readers witness the deep-seated prejudices and injustices that permeate the society of the time. As readers follow Scout's journey, they are challenged to question their own biases and beliefs about race and justice.

"Things Fall Apart" by Chinua Achebe. Set in pre-colonial Nigeria, the novel offers readers insight into the complexities of African cultures and the impact of colonialism on these societies. By the end of the novel, readers' assumptions about Africa and its peoples are challenged.

So it is novels that have the power to help us see the world in a different light, which is beneficial if readers want to broaden their perspectives. A novel has a wider canvas at its disposal that allows it to explore the complex relationships between individuals, families, and communities in the context of the country's socio-political reality. That alone can change readers' worldview and encourage them to think more deeply about the complexities of global issues, and help them break away from our confirmation biases.

Reading novels can also help us develop empathy and emotional intelligence. As we follow the characters through their journeys and struggles, we are able to connect with their emotions and experiences. This can help us become more attuned to the emotions of others in our own lives and develop greater empathy towards them.

In the same way, reading 1984 today can help us better understand contemporary politics and the ways in which governments around the world are using technology and surveillance to monitor their citizens. The novel's exploration of government overreach, propaganda, and censorship are particularly relevant in the age of social media and "fake news."

Rather than simply presenting us with facts and arguments, novels allow us to engage with complex issues and ideas in a way that is both accessible and emotionally engaging. In the case of 1984, the novel offers a vivid and disturbing portrayal of a society in which individuality and free thought are suppressed by an all-powerful government. Through the character of Winston Smith, we come to understand the human toll of living in such a society - the fear, the loneliness, the constant sense of being watched and controlled.

13
A Brief Chapter Wise Summary of 1984

Chapter 1-4:
The novel begins with the protagonist Winston Smith, a member of the Outer Party in the dystopian society of Oceania, beginning to question the authority of the ruling Party. Winston secretly purchases a diary, which is a thoughtcrime in the Party's totalitarian state, and begins to write about his dissent. He is haunted by his memories of a time before the Party's rise to power and longs for a life of freedom and autonomy. Winston meets a woman named Julia, with whom he begins a secret love affair.

Themes explored in these chapters: Totalitarianism, Oppression, Individualism, Rebellion, and Love.

Chapter 5-8:
Winston becomes increasingly disillusioned with

the Party and begins to express his discontent to Julia. Winston learns about the existence of a Brotherhood that opposes the Party's rule, and he begins to feel hopeful that change is possible. Winston also begins to read forbidden literature that challenges the Party's propaganda.

Themes explored in these chapters: Control through language, Surveillance, Manipulation of information, and the power of the past.

Chapter 9-12:

Winston's relationship with Julia deepens, and they begin to plan a rebellion against the Party. Winston is introduced to O'Brien, a high-ranking member of the Party whom Winston believes is a member of the Brotherhood. Winston and Julia are caught by the Party's Thoughtpolice, and they are taken to the Ministry of Love for interrogation and torture.

Themes explored in these chapters: Betrayal, Torture, Brainwashing, and the power of fear.

Chapter 13-18:

Winston is subjected to a grueling regimen of torture and brainwashing in the Ministry of Love. His will is gradually broken, and he is made to accept the Party's view of reality. He is finally released back into society, but he has been transformed into a loyal Party member who fully embraces the principles of Ingsoc.

Themes explored in these chapters: The power of propaganda, the malleability of truth, and the loss of individual identity.

Chapter 19-23:
Winston's transformation is complete, and he begins to actively participate in the Party's oppression of the population. Winston is reunited with Julia, but they both realize that they no longer love each other. Winston realizes that he has no hope of escaping the Party's control and that the Party's power is absolute.

Themes explored in these chapters: The cost of rebellion, the limits of individual freedom, and the nature of power.

Other Essays

1

Human Face vs Ideology: My Take on Elections

India's 2019 election was a spectacle of great pomp and show, but for many, it left behind a trail of disappointments and heartbreaks. Looking beyond the usual cycle of optimism and pessimism, there are many profound takeaways from the election results. Decades down the line, future generations searching for the leaders who shaped India's history will find no faces in the lavish galleries of Indian politics. Indian elections today propel faceless ideologies, with representational faces effacing and disappearing in the presence of the splendid sun of ideology.

Dehumanization has become the new norm shaping electoral politics worldwide, despite past repercussions. The abstract, obscure, inaccessible, and masked face of ideology has been given free rein, and chaos and confusion unsettle the judgment of the masses, creating a new omnipresent faceless face. Lok Sabha Elections 2019 were the battle between Human Face vs. Ideology, and ideology emerged victorious.

Ideology grips a larger chunk of the population under its spell and is all-encompassing. The human face is heir to small-scale appeal based on track record, work efficiency, and leadership ethics. Ideology is the most powerful of the two, and a sweeping victory like BJP's is not possible without a faceless face evoking profound reverence on the part of the masses.

History is replete with instances where ideological fronts rise, take shape, and let people go frenzy in the euphoria of being part of it, but all along the way, an ideology always breathes its own ruin. Time subjects ideologies to ruin over and again. In the tightly sealed mesh of unfound ideology, as masses suffocate, cracks ensue. The more centralization and unification on the ideological basis are sought, the more it hastens internal rebellion.

India is a land of diversity that cannot afford to fit everyone into one ideological shoe. The notorious example of Hitler's Germany's ideological unification cost humanity millions of innocent lives, billions of dollars in the economy, and above all, zillions of hopes and aspirations.

As long as ideology remains a driving force lurking behind the façade of chaos sand confusion, "Sabka Saath, Sabka Vikas" or the slogan of "equitable development" could not materialize into a reality. If free politics has to live, India must end the Liberal vs. Communal debate and fight to reclaim the precedence of the human face over anything else. The focus should be on eradicating the ideological earthquake that sends ripples to the far ends of the landmass and gives impunity to its adherents.

2

Pulwama Attack, Indian Muslims, and Nationalism

Political discourse in the immediate aftermath of the Pulwama attack instigated a pompous parade of nationalism, with politicians across the divide engaging in drumming it loud. The eruption of this volcano resulted in news anchors launching diatribes against the minority few, completely ignoring the fact that in the land of nationalists, nobody is nationalist enough. Even a slight deviance from the ruling dispensation's credo is enough to incur an anti-national label.

Since 2014, India has seen a proliferation of Prime Time factories that manufacture lies and invite panelists to be disgraced in front of millions, while labeling invitees as either nationalists or anti-nationalists depending on their stance. This monopoly of anchors has been challenged lately, with they themselves being disgraced in the same manner that they disgrace others.

This circus of antagonism masquerading as nationalism has led to the Indian Muslims being cornered to the wrong side of the divide, trying to prove their nationalism and avoid the wrath of the anchors by speaking against Pakistan in the wildest terms possible. However, this only highlights the lamentable fate that has pushed them into the fire.

One should not rush to prove one's nationalism and patriotism because the currents of nationalistic discourse offer no free entries. In such circumstances, it is best to keep a calm head and refrain from aligning with radical official discourse. After the Pulwama attack, a Muslim on Republic TV's 9 pm show was all fired up against Pakistan, demanding that India strike it in ten days' time. This 10-day ultimatum turned the debate towards Indian Muslims, with the anchor shouting at the speaker (who happened to be a Muslim) for doubting Army's capability by citing 10 days, not 10 hours.

The Kashmiri students, shopkeepers, and employees have been beaten up and humiliated, indicating that India is far from being an ideal democratic state. There are universities that have been denied aid and assistance because they refused to endorse the divisive ideology of the government and dared to dissent. The isolation of Pakistan has become a talking point in the mainstream media, with anchors giving verdicts on it with surprising confidence as if they are the ones running the theatrics of world politics.

Politics in India has become a circus that is dominated by nationalism and rhetoric that serves to divide people. It is high time that politicians and anchors stop this dangerous play and start treating everyone with respect and dignity. People's welfare is conjoined to their being treated equally and with the respect that they deserve.

In times of such uncertainty, it is important to exercise caution before hastily proclaiming nationalism and patriotism, as one can be labeled a nationalist in one moment and an anti-national in the next. Prime Minister Modi's late response to the violence against Kashmiri students had irked the international community, yet Omar Abdullah expressed gratitude for the PM's tweet condemning the attacks. It is puzzling how a simple tweet could undo the violence inflicted on innocent students.

Mehbooba Mufti, on the other hand, faced ridicule for her comments, which were seen as childish and irrational, suggesting relocating to Pakistan if India failed to isolate the former globally. She tried correcting herself by defending India, highlighting its democratic and secular nature while criticizing Pakistan as a rogue state that is undemocratic and radical. India is a thriving economy, but one has to question how much of its resources are being allocated to uplifting the poor and destitute, improving education and healthcare, generating new jobs, and providing basic amenities to all citizens. People are being lynched, jailed, tortured, or killed in India, yet she conveniently fails to mention the unbearable violence people go through. In this day and age, one can't afford to be a mouthpiece for despotic rulers. Rather, leaders should work towards addressing and resolving peoples' grievances, issues, and conflicts. Boasting about nationalism should not be the focus, as in a nation full of nationalists, no one is truly "nationalist enough."

3

Time's Conflicting Pulls

Every year, countless souls are tormented by the deadly play of politics, while the masses chase statistics, mistakenly believing that glaring figures represent progress. Blinded by these figures, they treat illusions, which are a mere contribution to a pool of stagnant waters, as a formidable force. However, the irony is that the water is already leaking, silently corroding the fragile walls of a confused nation.

Education fosters kindness and a sense of responsibility towards the underprivileged, replacing haste with contemplation. It eradicates impulsive reactions reminiscent of violent mobs, who kill, loot, plunder, and lynch people. Mobs fall for an easy bait and kill it and revel in their triumph. Ignorant and filled with xenophobia, they fail to grasp the complete picture of communal brutality. They remain unremorseful despite facing severe consequences resulting from their reckless actions. However, their prudence surfaces only when they are unexpectedly struck by a similar fate.

Our educational system may shine with a facade of brilliance, but beneath its colorful surface lies a nauseating lackluster and glaring darkness. Unsurprisingly then, the "educated" often prove to be more corrupt and untrustworthy. If not through the fissures of institutionalized education, how else does cunningness seep into the veins of the young? There is always a price to pay, for nothing comes without a cost. How can one claim to possess liberty? You enter the revered halls of democracy as innocent lambs and depart as wolves, consumed by violence, corruption, and a relentless pursuit of personal gain. Illiteracy holds no significance, as both the educated and illiterate share the same state of ignorance. Knowledge itself becomes ignorance, and ignorance becomes a source of power—an unsettling amalgamation.

Inside the classrooms of self-proclaimed intellectuals and pompous nationalists, the only discourse deemed valuable is one filled with mockery, vanity, and deceit. It is disheartening that the advancement of technology, with its high-resolution screens, fails to bring about the eradication of uncertainty. Any observant eye can witness that power and oppression bear no distinction, as slums and grand buildings emanate the same scent.

In the bewildering realm of universities and marketplaces, curious minds find themselves entangled. Houses of power and the cloaks worn by zealots paint sedition over the face of truth. A careful gaze reveals a recurring pattern of malevolent actions, venomous rhetoric, and despairing norms, where peace remains a scarce occurrence. Within the illusory walls of liberty, it is not the chains that are broken, but rather the sanity of individuals. With a slight detachment, one can witness the facade of democracy unravel, leaving behind a heap of crushed bones, devoid of the paradise it promised.

Within the confines of its four walls, true monsters unleash their mighty roars. And amidst them, a saint is thrown into the chaos. What choices does he have? Desperate, he will adapt. He will carve out a life for himself amidst the lifeless discourse. Even if it means transforming into a monster, he will confront the surrounding beasts and wolves. Engaging in a battle of roars will only taint the air with bitterness. Time is short, and there is much to conquer. Yet, he will prevail. He will master the art of political charlatanism, the brutality of those in power, the dishonesty of servants, the apathy of teachers, the scandals of self-proclaimed holy men, and the deceptive games of corporations.

Faithful to the pseudo-religion accuse secularists of intentionally diluting the religious character of their so-called "mighty" nation, perceiving it as a concealed conspiracy. However, between secularity and religiosity yonder lies humanity draped in tattered clothes.

PS: Let's envision a house with a water storage

unit, its contents reaching the brim. Water is consumed and replenished in a continuous cycle. However, prolonged exposure to harsh weather conditions has led to the development of cracks in the storage. As a result, seepage occurs, dampening the walls of the entire structure and putting the home at risk.

ABOUT THE AUTHOR

Shafqat Mushtaq holds a masters in English Literature from the University of Kashmir. Author of Spring Thoughts in Summer Light, Defy Odds and Be Unstoppable, JM Coetzee's Disgrace and Racism in Post-Apartheid South Africa, and more.

Contact Author: agogauthor@gmail.com

www.ingramcontent.com/pod-product-compliance
Lightning Source LLC
Chambersburg PA
CBHW031735150726
47989CB00006B/2462